Noisette Roses

19th Century Charleston's Gift to the World

Rosa Noisettiana.   Rosier de Philippe Noisette.

Edited by Virginia Kean
for the Charleston Horticultural Society
Charleston, South Carolina

Virginia Kean is a writer, editor, and producer based in Redwood City, California.

Charleston Horticultural Society
46 Windermere Blvd.
Charleston, South Carolina 29407

www.charlestonhorticulturalsociety.org

© 2009 by the Charleston Horticultural Society

All rights reserved. No part of this book may be reproduced in any form or
by any means, electronic or mechanical, including photocopying,
recording or by any information storage and retrieval system,
without written permission from the publisher.

Publisher Record Number: 1477728

1 3 5 7 9 8 6 4 2

FIRST PAPERBACK EDITION 2009

ISBN 978-0-615-25111-0 (paperback)

The Charleston Horticultural Society gratefully acknowledges the generous
contribution of the Heritage Rose Foundation to the production costs of this book.

Designed by Joan Olson

Printed in China through Global Interprint, Inc.
Santa Rosa, California

This book is printed on acid-free paper.

Title page illustration: *Rosa Noisettiana* by Pierre-Joseph Redouté
Inside back cover: 1825 Mills Atlas map of Charleston County

Contents

December 25, 2017

Rosemary,

We're so happy you were able to join us this year.

Merry Christmas!

Lee Batter & Joe Jitter

DEDICATION
Ruth C. Knopf

MANY ROSARIANS—Léonie Bell, the folks at Monticello, the proprietors of Vintage Gardens and the Antique Rose Emporium, and numerous people in Charleston, South Carolina—have made important contributions to the history, study, and promotion of the Noisette class of roses. But if one had to choose just one person who might be credited as the Noisette's "most faithful follower," the name of Ruth Knopf immediately comes to mind.

A native South Carolinian who has lived in the Charleston area for many years, Ruth has collected many "found" Noisettes and other heritage roses on her rose-rustling missions. And as good gardeners do, she propagated and shared these precious finds with her friends, often saving them from extinction.

Ruth was the driving force behind the 9th International Conference on Heritage Roses, held in Charleston in 2001, which celebrated this beautiful

and fascinating class of roses. In conjunction with the conference, Ruth led the development of the Hampton Park Noisette Study Garden and the Heritage Rose Trail in Charleston. Throughout the study of the Old Noisettes at Hampton Park, Ruth was at the center of the effort. She has a natural ability to observe a rose closely, to distinguish slight but significant variations between similar varieties, and to communicate these observations to others.

In 2005, Ruth was the first recipient of the Charleston Horticultural Society's prestigious 1830 Award for her great contributions to Charleston's horticultural heritage. And without her continued dedication and hard work, this book would surely not have been written. It is therefore with great delight that the editorial committee and all those involved in the production of this book dedicate it to Ruth Knopf.

For me rose growing is personal—if I grow it I love it. Thus my favorite Noisette is 'Rêve d'Or'. I planted it next to a cherry tree in London's Eccleston Square in 1990. Within five years it was hanging down from the top and now it's about 40 feet across and nearly as high as the tree can take it—about 24 feet. It bursts into flower around the middle of May and always amazes me.

—*Roger Phillips*

'Rêve d'Or' (photo by Roger Phillips)

WITH GLOBAL WARMING and periods of drought in the many parts of the world where Noisettes flourish, there can be no better time to launch a book on these remarkably resilient roses. And how fitting it is that the book is being published by the Charleston Horticultural Society of Charleston, South Carolina, where the original Noisette was created.

A couple of years ago I visited Charleston to attend the garden festival sponsored by the Charleston Horticultural Society and Middleton Place Foundation as the guest of Ruth Knopf, to whom this book is dedicated. Having met Ruth at many heritage rose conferences worldwide, I had come to realize that she is the authority on the Noisettes. During the festival, I was thrilled to see the great collections of Noisettes at Boone Hall, where Ruth is the garden consultant, and also at Hampton Park, and thoroughly enjoyed the Heritage Rose Trail tour of the historic old city of Charleston.

Ruth's love of the Noisettes is contagious and the collection she has amassed is extraordinary. The history of the first varieties, their spread to France, their rise in popularity and the breeding of the Tea-Noisettes, which brought rich yellows and apricots into the class, make for a fascinating story. This is a book that will be cherished by gardeners in the warmer areas of the world—the southern United States and California, South America, Australia, South Africa, New Zealand, the Mediterranean

Previous page: 1825 Mills Atlas map of Charleston County (courtesy of the South Carolina Historical Society)
Above: Boone Hall (photo by Phillip Robinson)

countries, India, and the Arab states—for many years to come.

The coauthors are a select group. They include historian John Meffert on what Charleston was like in the early nineteenth century when John Champneys bred the first Noisette; the late C. Patton Hash on the history of Champneys and his Noisette rose; rose nurseryman Gregg Lowery on the Old Noisettes and the promise they offered amateur gardeners and breeders alike in the nineteenth century; Ruth Knopf on her search for the Old Noisettes and on Charles-ton's Heritage Rose Trail; Malcolm Manners on the botanical characteristics of the Noisettes and the results of DNA comparison studies; Odile Masque-lier, president of *Association des Roses Anciennes en France*, on the beautiful Tea-Noisettes and why they are so garden-worthy; and JoAnn Breland on Charles-ton's Hampton Park and the Noisette Study Garden, which she oversees. In addition, an international cast of rose people—including Peter Beales and Roger Phillips of the UK, Gwen Fagan of South Africa, Bill Welch of Texas, Liesbeth Cooper of Bermuda, and Barbara Worl of California—describe their favorite Noisette rose. The editor is Virginia Kean, cofounder and editor in chief of *Rosa Mundi*, the journal of the Heritage Rose Foundation.

This much-needed work shines new light on the importance of this versatile group of roses and gives full credit to the original breeder, John Champneys of Charleston, South Carolina. Nearly two hundred years on from the introduction of 'Blush Noisette', the Noisette roses are finally getting the recognition they deserve.

—*David Ruston*
Chairman, Historic Roses Committee
World Federation of Rose Societies

ACKNOWLEDGMENTS

WHAT BEGAN AS AN ACADEMIC final report for a multiyear study of the roses at the Hampton Park Noisette Study Garden in Charleston, South Carolina, has blossomed into a publication for the entire world to enjoy. This book is the first to be published in America that is solely dedicated to an analysis of the Noisettes, a class of rose born in Charleston not long after the American Revolution.

Our challenge was to tell the story of this unique botanical contribution in a manner that would appeal to a wide audience—lovers of old roses and gardeners worldwide as well as Southern history buffs, admirers of historical Southern gardens, and the tourists who flock to Charleston to enjoy its beauty. What a task it has been to collect articles, photographs, historic images—everything needed to present the history of a type of rose that has not been celebrated nearly enough.

Committees have continued to work on the Noisette Study project at Hampton Park as well as the Heritage Rose Trail, which has enhanced our city from the Battery northward with hundreds of Noisette roses. The Noisette Study group worked diligently to raise funds to create and oversee the Noisette Study Garden and the Heritage Rose Trail, and finally to develop and publish this book.

There are so many people to thank. While there is always the danger of leaving someone out, two groups of people are especially deserving of our thanks. The Noisette Study project members are Malcolm

Manners, Maurice Thompson, JoAnn Breland, Ruth Knopf, Gregg Lowery, and Phillip Robinson. The Heritage Rose Trail has been under the care of Alice Levkoff, Harold Wade, Bob and Neltie Linker, JoAnn Breland, and Ruth Knopf, with the help of scores of volunteers.

Authors and contributors to whom we are especially grateful hail from all parts of the globe: South Africa, Australia, England, France, Bermuda, as well as the United States. To the South Carolina Historical Society we owe a special thanks for sharing the article by the late C. Patton Hash in the Spring 2000 issue of *Carologue* and to Mike Shoup of the Antique Rose Emporium, who allowed us to reprint his accompanying photographs. To Mike Coker of the South Carolina Historical Society, many thanks for researching historic images for the book. We also wish to thank Joyce Baker and the Gibbes Museum for permission to use Edward Savage's 1789 painting, *Mary Harvey Champneys and her Stepdaughter*.

Mary S. Miller, science reference librarian at the Charleston County Public Library, spent countless hours searching other libraries and special horticulture collections across the United States in an effort to determine whether this book is the very first book devoted solely to the study of the Noisette class of rose. Her research concluded that it is indeed the first of its kind to be published in America.

To the Heritage Rose Foundation, which is headed by Stephen Scanniello, go bouquets of Noisettes for a grant to publish fifteen hundred more copies of the book than originally planned, thereby making the cost of an individual book more affordable. This gift also enabled us to print the book in full color. The foundation's generosity is gratefully appreciated.

Lastly, to the Charleston Horticultural Society we present the proceeds of the sale of our publication so that they may continue their incredible efforts to achieve their mission to "inspire excellence in Lowcountry horticulture." We hope this book will become an integral part of the promotion and preservation of the Noisette class of roses, and help ensure their important place in both the history of the rose and of South Carolina.

—*Jane O. Waring*
Chairman, Publication Committee

—*Publication Committee Members:*
Mimi Cathcart, Malcolm Manners, Ruth Knopf, Gregg Lowery, John Meffert, and Jenny Gibbs

Previous page: 'Blush Noisette' (photo by Gregg Lowery)

CHAPTER ONE

Charleston in the Age of John Champneys

John Meffert

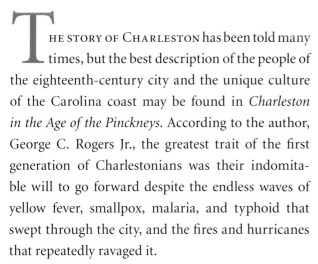

T HE STORY OF CHARLESTON has been told many times, but the best description of the people of the eighteenth-century city and the unique culture of the Carolina coast may be found in *Charleston in the Age of the Pinckneys*. According to the author, George C. Rogers Jr., the greatest trait of the first generation of Charlestonians was their indomitable will to go forward despite the endless waves of yellow fever, smallpox, malaria, and typhoid that swept through the city, and the fires and hurricanes that repeatedly ravaged it.

The Carolina colony was truly a new world for Dr. Alexander Garden, who arrived in Charles Town from Scotland in 1752 to practice medicine. His many letters to friends in Europe contain an Englishman's view of both the place and the people as he experienced them in the thirty years of his residence. Of the place he wrote:

> *Our long hot summers enervate and unbrace the whole system. Were you to sweat out, for two or three summers, the finer part of your good English blood and animal spirits and have every fiber and nerve of your body weakened, relaxed, enervated and unbraced by a tedious autumnal heat intermittent under a sultry suffocating and insufferable sun, you would then be made in some manner a judge of the reason for our taste or fire. . . . Instead of fire and life of imagination, indifference and a graceful despondency would overwhelm your mind.*

AFTER A DAY'S "PICKING."

Previous page: View of Charleston from the harbor, ca. 1780
Above: Nineteenth-century engraving of cotton workers
returning from the fields
Right: View of a Field at Woodstock Under Harvest,
watercolor by Charles Fraser, 1782–1860
(all courtesy of the South Carolina Historical Society)

Of the people he observed in a letter to a friend in London:

> *. . . In Charles Town we are a set of the busiest most bustling hurrying animals imaginable, and yet we really do not do much but we must appear to be doing. And this kind of important hurry appears among all ranks, unless among the gentleman planters who are absolutely above every occupation but eating, drinking, smoking and sleeping which five modes of action constitute the essence of their life and existence.*

Dr. Garden's views, however, would not have been shared by the natives of Charles Town for in the seventy years from the founding of the colony, the planters had transformed the natural landscape into one of the most productive agricultural regions in the world. By 1750, Charles Town's merchants were trading around the globe—from Africa to the West Indies to the European continent. They were entrepreneurial spirits who imagined a new society based on an English model. John Champneys, who is credited with the development of the first Noisette rose, was typical of the type.

From 1720 to 1760, plantation agriculture expanded exponentially. The establishment of the royal colonial government in 1721 provided security for the influx of Englishmen from the Barbados and French Huguenots, Scots Irish, Swiss, and German Protestants from the Palatinate. All participated in creating the new economic order.

In her book *Historical Atlas of the Rice Plantations of the Ace River Basin—1860*, historian Suzanne Cameron Linder writes that plantation agriculture was conceived by the vision of men from London who "harnessed the sun and the moon, and turned the marshes into fields of gold." The landscape itself was shaped by the hands of Africa. The planters enslaved Africans who came from West Africa with centuries of knowledge and experience in growing rice. Land allotments given for head rights for each slave also helped the planters acquire more plantation lands.

By 1745 the end of the monopoly of the Royal Africa Company opened the slave trade to American traders. After 1745 the introduction of indigo, a new crop that was heavily dependent on slaves, made slavery even more indispensable. As one contemporary observer wrote, the combination of these factors insured that "Carolina looks more like a Negro country than a country inhabited by whites."

John Champneys was born in Charles Town in 1743 to a royal colonial official. He grew up in a landscape that was rapidly being transformed from "a country inferior to none in fertility and abounding in variety of the blessings of nature," as botanist Mark Catesby described it in the 1720s, to one based on a new pattern—plantation agriculture. Champ-

neys witnessed these changes, and as a young man he benefited from them. By the 1760s he was a successful factor on the Charles Town docks. By 1763 he had married Ann Livingston and bought property on the Charles Town Neck where he intended to raise a family far from the bustle of the city.

Champneys' rise to fortune coincided with the age of the great sailing ships. Charles Town's location on the Great Atlantic Highway made the port a major entry point. By 1760 Edmund Burke observed that "the only town in either of the Carolinas which can draw attention is Charles Town . . . it is one of the first in North America for size, beauty and traffic." Most of the early merchants who achieved success dreamed of returning to England to buy a country estate and join the gentry. Champneys, however, wanted his family to become new gentry in America.

Above: Charleston Light Dragoon,
watercolor by Charles Fraser, 1782–1860
Right: Woodville The Seat of R. Beresford Esquire,
watercolor by Charles Fraser, 1782–1860
(both courtesy of the South Carolina Historical Society)

By 1760 the land was secure, the Indians had been subdued, and the Spanish were no longer a threat. The city was being transformed as well. Handsome brick structures were replacing the old wooden city. Josiah Quincy, a Boston merchant who visited the city in 1773, found Charles Town impressive. Of the place he wrote "the number of shipping far surpassed all I had ever seen in Boston . . . the town struck me very agreeably, but the New Exchange which fronted the place made a most noble appearance." Of the society he wryly noted that "all seems to be trade, riches, magnificence and great state in everything . . . much gaiety and dissipation." But the aspirations of the people in the early 1770s were best expressed in the Charles Town Gazette of the period. Speaking of men such as John Champneys, the editors wrote:

> *Their whole lives are one continual race in which everyone is endeavoring to distance all behind him, and to overtake or pass by all before him. Every tradesman is a merchant, every merchant is a gentleman, and every planter is one of the noblesse. We are a country of gentry; we have no such thing among us as common people. Between vanity and fashion the species is utterly destroyed!*

For Champneys and others in Charles Town, the concept of a society based on the English gentry model was soon to be overthrown. The revolutionary period became a nightmare for Champneys and his family. In 1776 after refusing to take an oath to support the new state of South Carolina, he was arrested as a Loyalist, tried, convicted and imprisoned. After being held in jails in Charles Town, Georgetown, and Cheraw, South Carolina, he was banished from Charles Town and ordered to leave within sixty days. Confined by a court order to his plantation, he was helpless to act as his goods and furniture were auctioned in the city.

Champneys petitioned the state assembly for leniency but his appeal was unsuccessful. In 1777 he boarded a ship for France with his wife, two children, a Negro servant, 15 pounds sterling and his family portraits, leaving behind property valued at 20,000 pounds sterling. In 1778 he published a pamphlet describing his mistreatment:

The following pages are a true and genuine account of the sufferings and persecution of the subscriber by a part of the American bunch of Kings, those pretenders to liberty, but at the same time exercising such tyrannical and oppressive actions as ought to make those peoples who style themselves their friends ashamed.

As C. Patton Hash describes in Chapter 2 in more detail, Champneys' tribulations had just begun. With the fall of Savannah in 1779 he attempted to sail back to Georgia, but his ship was waylaid by pirates and he ended up in Bermuda. There his wife died. When he set sail again, his ship was once more waylaid by privateers. This time he ended up in Philadelphia. There one of his two remaining children died. He finally reached British-occupied Charles Town in 1781. He then sought to reclaim his property, without success. Champneys remarried and began life anew but was forced to flee again in 1783 when the British finally abandoned the city. He returned to London and remained there until his claim for restitution as a loyal subject was settled by the Crown. He received only 5,000 pounds sterling.

After the revolution, the planters held sway in the city, whose name had been changed from Charles Town to Charleston. By 1790 Champneys was back again in Charleston. Although his banishment had been expunged, he was branded a traitor and never achieved the success of the pre-war period. He retreated to the country village of Rantowles. By 1796 he had purchased the plantation of William

Williamson, known as The Garden. Here he pursued life as a country gentleman and developed a 10-acre pleasure ground and nursery.

In *Letters from an American Farmer*, Hector Crevecoeur observed that the "three principal classes of inhabitants [of Charleston] are planters, lawyers, and merchants . . . this is the province which has afforded the first the richest spoils, for nothing can exceed their wealth, their power and their influence." By the early 1800s Charleston was a wealthy enclave for a new aristocracy dominated by planters whose coffers were filled by profits from a new crop—cotton. In 1809 historian

Above: Rare sketch of Saint Philip's Church by Thomas You, ca. 1766 (courtesy of the South Carolina Historical Society)

David Ramsay wrote this of the people: "the planters have large incomes, live at their ease, enjoy much, and suffer little. They are high minded and possess much of the dignity and character of independent country gentlemen, but seldom engage in any arduous pursuits to the accomplishment of which much time, patience and long continued exertion are necessary."

But by the early nineteenth century, one problem confronted all the planters in the Lowcountry—the exhaustion of the land itself. Of the place Ramsay wrote that "the bulk of the planters rely on the fertility of the soil, changing land when it begins to fail and seldom bother to keep their fields in heart. Though deriving great profit from indigo, rice, and cotton, the planters have always neglected the garden." The failing land finally forced John Champneys to relocate his family to new land on the Georgia Coast.

On his departure from The Garden, Champneys sent the fruits of his plantation nursery to the newly formed Charleston Botanical Garden, operated by Philippe Noisette. By 1810 he had faded from the Charleston scene. In 1820 Champneys passed away in the bosom of his family at Champneys Island, Georgia. However, as a good native son of Carolina he was buried in Saint Philip's Churchyard in Charleston. His family continued to live on Champneys Island until the Civil War when, once again, the family lost everything that Champneys had held dear.

C H A P T E R   T W O

Champneys and South Carolina's Forgotten Rose

C. Patton Hash

SOUTH CAROLINA IS A LAND of gardens. Blessed with fertile soil and mild winters, South Carolinians have from the earliest days cultivated and tended gardens that with their azaleas, camellias, and jessamine draw visitors from throughout the world. Yet one plant reigns over all others as the Queen of Flowers—the rose. Throughout the state, roses bloom in nearly every garden, almost without ceasing. Few people, however, know the essential role that South Carolina played in the development of the rose.

In the eighteenth century, the United States was proving a lucrative market for English nurserymen, and South Carolina, already noted for its gardens and warm climate, was becoming a major center for the importation of plant material, particularly from Asia. Colonial gardens in the newly settled Carolina faced summers that lasted from May until October. Many plants suffered in the humidity and tropical heat, among them the once-blooming old European roses.

The first remontant (ever-blooming) rose was introduced to Britain about 1793. Known as 'Old Blush', 'Common Monthly', or the 'China Rose', it probably arrived at Kew Gardens near London from Calcutta, where it had been imported from Canton in southeast China. But little could be done in Britain's cool climate to develop this Asian rose's potential. It was in the more welcoming environment of South Carolina that this rose would thrive and bear fruit.

Historic Background

John Champneys was born on December 28, 1743, the son of John Champneys, a government official in

Page 7: 'Champneys' Pink Cluster' (photo by Ruth Knopf)
Left: Detail of Mary Harvey Champneys and her Stepdaughter,
1789, by Edward Savage (American, 1761–1817). Oil on canvas.
© Image Gibbes Museum of Art/Carolina Art Association
1937.002.0002
Above: Engraving of Charleston, South Carolina's waterfront, 1742
(courtesy of the South Carolina Historical Society)

royal South Carolina, and his wife Mary Musgrove. He married Ann Livingston in 1763 and by the time of the Revolutionary War was a successful factor and wharfinger. During the War, Champneys remained loyal to the Crown, an allegiance for which he would

Above: Rosa moschata *by Pierre-Joseph Redouté*
Right: 'Old Blush' *(photo by Malcolm Manners)*

suffer greatly. He left South Carolina in 1777, sailed for London, and lived there until the capture of Savannah in 1779. In 1778 he published *An Account of the Persecution and Sufferings of John Champneys*, which details his ordeal in the first year of the War. In 1779 Champneys and his family sailed for Savannah after its occupation by the British. His ship was captured and he was taken to Bermuda, where his wife died. He then attempted to sail back to Charleston, but his vessel was again seized and taken to Philadelphia, where one of his children died. On his third attempt, he arrived in Charleston with his last surviving child. He soon remarried, resumed his business, but then had to evacuate to St. Augustine, Florida, when the British retired from Charleston in 1782. He returned to Charleston in 1783 and waited fifteen months for the South Carolina legislature to lift his confiscation and banishment. His appeal failed and he was forced to leave Charleston yet again.

In 1786 Champneys was living in London on Fleet Street, but by 1790 he was back in Charleston. In 1796 he purchased an estate south of Charleston that had been developed by William Williamson. Lying on the road between Charleston and Jacksonborough and fronting on the Wallace River, the Williamson property was well known for its beauty and gardens. In his 1809 *History of South Carolina*, historian David Ramsay describes it thus:

Above: A Distant View of Charleston, *watercolor by Charles Fraser, 1782–1860 (courtesy of the South Carolina Historical Society)*
Right: 'Blush Noisette' (photo by Mike Shoup)

What was one of the most elaborate early gardens was in St. Paul's district and was formerly owned by William Williamson, but now belongs to John Champneys. It contains 26 acres, six of which are sheets of water and abound in excellent fish; ten acres in pleasure grounds are planted in every species of flowering trees, shrubs and flowers that this and the neighboring states can furnish: also with similar curious productions from Europe, Asia, and Africa.

Sometime after purchasing the Williamson plantation, probably between 1800 and 1814, Champneys developed a rose that was a hybrid of 'Old Blush' (*Rosa chinensis*), and the 'Musk Rose' (*Rosa moschata*). Unlike its European cousins, this vigorous rose with its white single or double flowers, which are borne in clusters on arching shoots, blooms in late spring and continues flowering into late autumn. The new rose, called 'Champneys' Pink Cluster', is the first rose in the western world to be truly remontant, or ever-blooming. This is the ancestor of the class of roses called the Noisettes. 'Champneys' Pink Cluster' launched an era of rose development that continues to this day.

Origins of Champneys' New Rose

When did Champneys develop the cross between the 'Musk Rose' and 'Old Blush'? From whom did he get his original plants? The simplest answer is that both parent roses were already growing on William Williamson's plantation when Champneys purchased it in 1796. But in the case of 'Old Blush', this is unlikely because the first written record of that rose in the United States appears in the 1799 catalogue of William Prince, a nurseryman in Flushing, New York. So it seems highly probable that Prince was the source for Champneys' plants of both roses. Indeed in a later account, Prince's son reported the following:

> *The original variety is the Champney Rose, or Champneys' Pink Cluster, a rose long well known and very widely diffused. It was raised from seed by the late John Champney, Esq. [sic] Of Charleston, S.C., an eminent and most liberal votary of Flora, from the seed of the White Musk Rose, or Rosa Moschata, fertilized by the old Blush China, and as he had been for a long period in constant correspondence with the late William Prince, he most kindly presented him with two tubs, each containing six plants, grown from cuttings of the original plant.*

Another possible source for Champneys' parent plants was John Fraser, one of the most colorful botanist-explorers of the day. Born in Scotland and trained at Kew, Fraser arrived in South Carolina in 1786 and by 1787 had published *Flora Caroliniana*, the first extensive study of the state's flora and a landmark in American botanical writing. Fraser started a nursery on the Stono River near where Maybank Highway crosses onto John's Island. Only a few miles separated it from Champneys' plantation on the Wallace River, a tributary of the Stono. A rose named 'Blush Musk', "Fraser's Pink Musk," or *Rosa fraserii*, was developed at the same

'Blush Noisette' (photo by Étienne Bouret)

'Blush Noisette', also known as 'Noisette Carnée', is probably my favorite Noisette. First, it is a really perpetual bloomer, generously flowering until the frost in Lyon and all through the year in Southern France. Exhaling the typical fruity fragrance of the first Noisette, 'Noisette Carnée' can be grown as a large shrub or a small climber.

In the park of Schloss Arenenberg (Arenenberg Castle) overlooking Switzerland's Lake Constance, I have seen a long pergola entirely covered with 'Blush Noisette'. On a very warm day in early June, we were visiting the Schloss, the final home of Empress Joséphine's daughter Queen Hortense, but walking under this pergola was deliciously fresh and moving.

—*Odile Masquelier*

time as 'Champneys' Pink Cluster', and John Champneys could very well have been the breeder. Fraser also imported plants to America. An advertisement he placed in the local gazette is the first written record of 'Old Blush', one of the parent roses, in Charleston:

> *J. Fraser at Mr. A. Duncan's, Queen Street, No. 113, has for sale—two new kinds of Evergreen perpetually Flowering Roses, originally from the East Indies; one kind bears dark crimson coloured Flowers, the other pale red Flowers. Those incomparable Roses, are well established in Garden pots, and are in a handsome state of vegetation.*

Noisette—the Story Behind the Name

Why is the class of reblooming roses descended from Champneys' landmark new rose called the Noisettes? One assumption has been that Champneys lacked the talent or interest to develop the rose further. Another story is that Philippe Stanislas Noisette, a French-born nurseryman based in Charleston, provided both of the roses from which Champneys made his cross, and that Champneys gave Noisette the rose.

Philippe Noisette was the son of Joseph Noisette, a gardener to the nobility of France prior to the French Revolution. He is said to have arrived in Charleston in 1795 from the island of Saint-Domingue (now Haiti), but appears in no historic records until 1808 when he is mentioned in the minutes of the Charleston Botanical Society as its director. The city directory of 1809 lists him as living in Hampstead. For most of his life, Noisette maintained a residence and nursery on Charleston Neck.

Noisette probably came to Charleston for two reasons. First, as the city had a well-established reputation in the botanical field, Noisette undoubtedly thought he could develop a business there. Secondly, the city offered a network of support based on his connections with the French émigré community from Saint-Domingue, which would provide a footing for eventual success. One of Noisette's influential friends, Dr. Joseph Johnson, was the driving force behind the founding of the Botanical Society, which established a botanical garden in Charleston in 1805. When they hired Noisette as director in 1808, the Society faced significant difficulties. A lottery that was to pay for improvements to the botanical garden proved a failure and in the Society's minutes for 1810, the land was reported as being sterile. The Society tried to move the botanical garden to land owned by William Turpin on Charleston Neck, but the effort failed and the Society and its garden disappeared.

By the time this happened, Noisette was a successful nurseryman with land on Charleston Neck along present-day Rutledge Avenue, which he had purchased from a merchant named Nathaniel Russell. Until the middle of the twentieth century, the property remained in the Noisette family as a nursery. In 1814 Noisette sent a rose specimen to his brother Louis Claude, a nurseryman in France, where appreciation for this Champneys-type rose became intense. The class of rose was named after Philippe Noisette when Louis Claude invited Pierre-Joseph Redouté, the most famous flower painter of the nineteenth century, to depict the rose, which was 'Blush Noisette'. On his painting of 'Blush Noisette', Redouté wrote the words *Rosa Noisettiana* and *Rosier de Philippe Noisette*. This image was reproduced throughout the world and thus the name "Noisette" became well known.

Development of the Noisette Class

'Blush Noisette' is a more refined rose than 'Champneys' Pink Cluster'. William Prince described it as "more double than its parent, and of much more dwarf and compact growth; the flowers in very large dense panicles." Prince was not so kind to Noisette. He wrote that "the origin of the first varieties of this remarkable group has been announced erroneously to the world by various writers, arising first from the want of candor on the part of Philippe Noisette of Charleston when he transmitted the plants to Paris; and secondly, from the ignorance of those who have discussed the subject." Yet he gives proper credit to

'Lamarque' (photo by Mike Shoup)

the class: "Perhaps no new roses ever excited more attention than the two varieties which were first produced of this interesting family. When first received in France, the Parisian amateurs were enraptured with it, its habits being so peculiar and distinct from every other class."

After 1814, further development of the Noisette class occurred far from the coast of South Carolina. The next step was the crossing of 'Blush Noisette' with the latest arrivals from Asia, the Tea roses. The introduction of the Teas transformed the Noisette class, enlarging the blooms, altering the scent, and lessening the tendency to bloom in large clusters. Ironically, in South Carolina and throughout the South, Tea roses became more popular than Noisettes. Some varieties of Noisettes continued to be planted, particularly 'Cloth of Gold' and 'Lamarque', but the earliest Noisettes fell from fashion and were soon to be found only in old farmyards and cemeteries.

Champneys and the End of an Era

Champneys died in 1820, just a few years after 'Blush Noisette' was introduced in France. He is buried in the eastern side of St. Philip's Churchyard, immediately south of the church. Philippe Noisette lived for nearly twenty years after the introduction of the rose named for him. He continued to operate his nursery, which became a required stop on tours of Charleston. Noisette died in 1835. In his will he left his "herbarium and collection of snakes and insects in bottles to the administrators of the Garden and Royal Museum of Natural History at Paris." His books and a few plants were given to Dr. Vincent Leseigneur, an old and devoted friend. He asked that his medals and papers along with a collection of seeds indigenous to the southern United States be sent to his brothers Lewis and Antoine. Most importantly, he granted freedom to his wife Celestine and their children, and left them enough to leave the state. Noisette is buried in an unmarked grave in the churchyard of St. Mary's Roman Catholic Church in Charleston.

Williamson's Garden, the estate of John Champneys south of Charleston, has not survived the ravages of time. Today nothing remains of the 26 acres described by historian David Ramsay. The ponds, the pleasure grounds, and the extensive plantings are all gone. By the end of the antebellum period, no mention is made of the Garden in any account. The era of phosphate mining sealed its fate. The land was stripped and the last vestiges of the pride of Champneys passed away. Today cars hurry by on their way from Charleston to points south. Sadly, no marker stands to tell the story of a truly historic site. A revolution in gardening occurred here, but only a street sign designates Champneys Lane—all else is lost to time.

And what of the roses, 'Champneys' Pink Cluster' and 'Blush Noisette'? They bloom on, lasting memorials to their creators. Progenitors of nearly every rose known today, they have spread one of the glories of the gardens of our beloved Palmetto State throughout the world. ❧

EDITOR'S NOTE: *This chapter was first published as an article in* Carologue, *a publication of the South Carolina Historical Society. The Charleston Horticultural Society is grateful to the South Carolina Historical Society for permission to edit and reprint it.*

"Bermuda Kathleen" (photo by Gregg Lowery)

As soon as I first saw "Bermuda Kathleen," I fell in love with it as I am especially fond of single and semidouble flowers. The large clusters of small, delicate, pastel-colored blooms are absolutely delightful. They open from slightly pointed buds to pale peachy-pink, then deepen in color to pink and finally to dark pink with prominent yellow stamens much like 'Mutabilis'. We in the Bermuda Rose Society suspect that "Bermuda Kathleen" is a chance seedling of 'Mutabilis'.

Having originated in past president Mrs. Hilda Horsfield's garden, the rose has been grown all around Bermuda for about sixty years. It grows into an open shrub with lax canes and delicate, dark green foliage. It can be grown as a specimen plant but looks wonderful against a Bermuda limestone wall where it will easily reach 6 to 8 feet in height and 6 feet in width. Flower arrangers love to use the clusters of small light-orange hips.

—*Liesbeth Cooper*

CHAPTER THREE

Introducing the Old Noisettes

Gregg Lowery

WHEN WE LOOK AT the Old Noisette roses today, with their small, scented blooms in delicate sprays of pale tinting, they seem perhaps old-fashioned. It is difficult to imagine how fresh and new and exciting they were two hundred years ago, and how they may have represented a wonderful new world to gardeners of that time.

The first Noisette, 'Champneys' Pink Cluster', might have been a chance of nature or may have been an intentional cross by Charleston's John Champneys. But no matter what its actual origin, there can be little doubt that it was a new rose—unique, beautiful, and garden-worthy. A rose of sweet perfume, it flowers in large clusters of small blooms, building into a tidy upright shrub and offering soft blush buds from early spring until well into winter.

Its parents were the China rose, 'Old Blush', and the old 'Musk Rose', presumably the single-flowered *Rosa moschata*, which was familiar to gardeners in Colonial America. A small ever-blooming shrub rose, 'Old Blush' was a new introduction to Europe and America from Asia in the mid to late eighteenth century. It was one of four roses from Asia that when hybridized with the old European roses led to modern roses as we know them. The 'Musk Rose' was a robust shrub with handsome gray-green foliage and large clusters of very fragrant white blooms. It begins blooming somewhat later than many other roses but then flowers continuously until late autumn.

Amateur gardeners in Europe and America must have been excited at the potential that the new roses from Asia held for their gardens. These rather tender musk and China roses provided a season of blossom that could last six months or more of the year, especially in warm climates. They thrived in the mild winter climate of Charleston, South Carolina, where amateur horticulturists like John Champneys could grow them to perfection. Their progeny, the American Noisettes, changed the direction of rose breeding in Europe in a profound way. The promise that lay in these fragrant reblooming shrubs was not lost on European breeders. Roses commonly grown in nineteenth-century gardens were the spring-flowering, once-blooming Gallicas, Damasks, Centifolias, and small-flowered Ramblers. The arrival of the China and Tea-scented roses did not really expand that selection, except in the milder climates of Southern Europe. Champneys' Noisette rose offered the first breakthrough in combining European once-bloomers with the ever-blooming roses of the Orient, and it was hardy enough for Northern European gardens.

In the first Noisette roses, the subtle coloring of the pink Chinas and their robust, compact habit tem-

Previous page: 'Blush Noisette' (photo by Mike Shoup)
Left: 'Climbing Old Blush' (photo by Barbara Worl)
Right: William Robert Prince (courtesy The Standard Cyclopaedia of Horticulture, *Liberty Hyde Bailey, London, 1917)*

pered and softened the vigorous nature of the 'Musk Rose', while it endowed them with large flower clusters and a hardier nature than the China roses. According to the American nurseryman William Robert Prince (1795–1869), more roses in the style of 'Champneys' Pink Cluster' were introduced in a short period following the introduction of the original seedling. Prince's father, William Prince (1766–1842), had corresponded with John Champneys, who "most kindly presented him with two tubs each containing six plants, grown from cuttings of the original plant."

William Robert Prince wrote that many plants "were propagated and sent to England and France" from these gift plants. He also noted that Philippe Noisette's seedling rose 'Blush Noisette' was raised a few years later, and that it was a less prolific seed parent—all of which suggests that more seedlings were raised from the original 'Champneys' Pink Cluster'. By 1846 Prince lists roughly seventy named varieties of these old Noisettes in his nursery catalogue. Many were of American or British origin; many more came from French breeders.

When the first Champneys' type Noisette arrived in Europe, breeders began raising seed from and making crosses with this delightful new rose. While many seedlings resembled the Old Noisettes, crosses with Tea roses inevitably created a new strain of Noisettes with larger flowers borne in smaller clus-

ters in a wider range of colors. The first of this new strain, 'Lamarque', was introduced in 1830. By 1846 William Robert Prince was arguing that the Noisette class needed subdividing. Writing that the "simple title of Noisette cannot at present convey a correct idea of the numerous discordant varieties which are now embraced under this head," Prince suggested that a separate classification for the large-flowered types was needed, and perhaps even another group for those of very small stature.

Prince's large list of named Noisettes of the Champneys' type is accompanied with brief descrip-

Above: Rosa moschata flore semi-pleno *(illustration by Redouté)*
Right: 'Blush Noisette' *(photo by Étienne Bouret)*

tions that are by no means sufficient for the task of identifying the cultivars we now grow. For example, he describes the Noisette rose 'Castalie' as "a variety, of a delicate flesh color, very distinct and pretty." That description, considering how similar the Old Noisettes are and how limited their range of colors, can easily apply to the tints found in more than half of the Noisettes available today. And while we may long to know the original name of one of the found Noisettes that have been discovered in old Southern gardens and cemeteries, like "Cato's Cluster," finding proof for any name would be daunting. The horticultural sources of the time simply don't provide the needed information.

Many of the early Noisettes that have surfaced in old gardens in the United States may have been seed-raised by amateur gardeners. The difference between a plant propagated from seed and one raised from cuttings was not altogether understood by nineteenth-century gardeners, and even today is often not understood. A named Noisette cultivar like 'Blush Noisette' could only be replicated by cloning—taking stem or root tissue from the mother plant and encouraging it to grow into a new plant. A seedling would have been a new and unique cultivar, deserving of its own name.

Gardeners in the early nineteenth century may well have taken seed from a plant of 'Blush Noisette', grown it on and considered the new plant 'Blush

Top: Hybrid Musk 'Penelope' (photo by Ron Robertson)
Above: "Cato's Cluster" (photo by Gregg Lowery)

Noisette.' But plants propagated from seed are not exact replicas of their parents. As for self-sown seedlings of the Old Noisettes, they are very similar to the early Champneys' type, but this superficial similarity does not make them the same plant as the rose from whose seed they came. Think of the Old Noisettes in nineteenth-century America, if you will, as a *strain* of roses. Even the least skilled of gardeners could obtain and grow them in their gardens either from seed or from cuttings. And they didn't vary much, so they were *all* in a sense 'Blush Noisette' or 'Champneys' Pink Cluster'.

Nonetheless, many nineteenth-century gardeners had a sophisticated awareness of the differences between cultivars of roses. Prince would not have offered seventy different named Old Noisette types had there not been some sort of market for them. Rose collectors then were not unlike rose collectors today who find joy in the subtle shades of difference between roses.

Much has been made of the simple beauty of early Noisettes like 'Champneys' Pink Cluster' and its offspring 'Blush Noisette'. But the Noisette class was to evolve in new and beautiful directions as European rose breeders began to hybridize the early Noisettes with large-flowered Tea roses. Their crosses increased the color range and created the first group of everblooming climbing roses—the Tea-Noisettes, whose popularity led to the neglect and eventual eclipsing of the Old Noisettes. Many nineteenth-century authors seem to agree that something wonderful was lost when the class became noticeably influenced by the Tea roses.

Early in the twentieth century a British rose breeder, Reverend Joseph Pemberton, put his hand to creating a new race of roses inspired by the roses in his mother's garden, old cluster-flowering roses like the Noisettes. Pemberton's new group came to be known as the Hybrid Musks. Their charm lay in the uncomplicated style of the flowers, their fragrance and profusion, and their continuity of bloom—all qualities that made them romantic inhabitants of the garden. Their very name evoked the fragrant 'Musk Rose' of ancient gardens, and they were descended from the Old Noisettes they sought to emulate.

In the coming years I can imagine controversy arising as to which rose is the *true* 'Champneys' Pink Cluster'. But all foundling Noisettes are 'Champneys' Pink Cluster' in a sense. They are all of that original old strain which two hundred years ago was so striking, new and revolutionary, so full of promise, so American.

'Champneys' Pink Cluster' (photo by Gregg Lowery)

Having lived in historic Charleston my entire life, it seems only natural that I should choose the earliest Noisette as my favorite rose. Named for Charlestonian John Champneys, father of the Noisette class of roses, 'Champneys' Pink Cluster' in my garden is very remontant. Its clusters of delicate pale pink petals combined with the loveliest fragrance in the old rose world would enhance the beauty of any garden.

—*Mimi Cathcart*

With so many lovely Noisette roses back in commerce, I should probably name 'Rêve d'Or' or 'Mme Alfred Carrière' as my favorite, but I can't resist the opportunity to share my enthusiasm for a "found" rose of questionable origins that I believe should be much more widely known. I first came across it while visiting with my wife's grandmother in Natchitoches, Louisiana, in about 1983.

"Natchitoches Noisette" (photo by Gregg Lowery)

Natchitoches (pronounced Nak-uh-tish) is considered by some historians to be the oldest city in the Louisiana Purchase, and is certainly one of the most beautiful. Alluvial soils from the Cane River, the city's favored location in the west central part of the state, and adequate rainfall provide excellent growing conditions. Not surprisingly, the city's cemetery, which includes graves dating to the late 1600s, has been a favorite haunt of rose collectors for many years.

I too wandered there in search of roses. In a partially shaded area of the graveyard that wasn't close enough to a headstone to relate it to a particular individual, I found an interesting plant with a few blossoms. It seemed a bit like 'Old Blush' but there are subtle differences in its fragrance, foliage, and the coloration of the flowers. I liked it and took cuttings, which rooted easily and were shared with The Antique Rose Emporium. Since then, it has stood the test of time well and remains a favorite. A 4 to 6 foot tall specimen to the right of the entrance of my house gets good sun and blooms almost continuously from mid spring until hard frost. Its healthy foliage, fragrance, and vigor are welcome in my garden and make me wonder about its past. I have never been tempted to adopt a "real" name for it by anything I have seen or read in the literature. Thankfully, it is available from several commercial sources.

—**William (Bill) C. Welch**

CHAPTER FOUR

Rediscovering the Old Noisettes

Ruth Knopf

Y STORY WITH THE ROSES began in 1970. In planning a new garden for my then home in upstate South Carolina, I decided to plant only my favorite plants, the ones I really loved. As I made the list, a rose that I remembered from my childhood growing up in South Carolina came to mind. It was a rose with small pink blooms having only five petals. I could not find this rose in local nurseries and soon learned that it was probably what was called an "old rose."

Where would I find roses such as these? During our family's traditional vacation at the beach that summer, we made our annual trek to nearby Pawley's Island Hammock Shop. There on a five dollar sales table lay a book titled *Wild and Old Garden Roses* by Gordon Edwards. On its beautiful dust jacket was the

old Gallica rose 'Rosa Mundi' with white foxgloves. I read and studied this book all winter and wanted every rose in it!

Another valuable find was the catalogue of the nursery Roses of Yesterday and Today. It contained wonderful descriptive lists of old roses as well as references to a catalogue of old rose books offered by Bell's Book Store in Palo Alto, California. At Bell's, book buyer Barbara Worl specialized in these and other old garden books. Another reference in *Roses of Yesterday*

Previous page: "Fewell's Noisette" (photo by Gregg Lowery)
Above: Ruth Westwood's garden (photo by Ruth Knopf)
Right: Herbert Bell and Barbara Worl at Bell's Book Store in
Palo Alto, California, ca. 1960s (photo courtesy of Faith Bell)
Far right: "Tutta's Mountain Cabin Noisette"
(photo by Ruth Knopf)

and Today was to a newly formed subscription group called The Rose Letter. I immediately joined it and sent off for the catalogue of old rose books from Bell's Book Store. I also learned of nurseries, such as Georgia's Thomasville Rose Nursery, that specialized in old roses. The Charleston Library Society also proved to be an invaluable resource that provided access to wonderful collections of garden books.

The following spring I was invited to visit the rose garden of a longtime collector of old roses, the late Ruth Westwood, a spry and witty lady who lived in Newberry, South Carolina, some 65 miles from my home. It was in her garden that I saw for the first time, in person, roses I had only read about. There they were in their many enchanting forms and colors: red and white striped ones, pink and white roses climbing on fences and arbors, a large bushy rose with clusters of tiny pink pompom blossoms, and dozens of others. At the end of my visit that day, Mrs. Westwood invited me to come back for cuttings and a lesson in rooting these roses. Telling me how she rooted everything in a big washtub over the winter and had good luck, she promised me cuttings of everything I wanted. Her invitation had me on my way to wonderful days ahead of finding and growing roses. From that day forward, when I saw a rose I liked on someone's fence or in their garden, I just stopped and asked for a cutting.

Into my garden of favorite plants these first tiny rooted roses went. Soon they were joined by other roses that I rooted from those I began to find growing in cemeteries and old churchyards around Charleston, like that of the first Unitarian church in the south, which is located in the city. In its elegant and crumbling cemetery is a garden rampant with beautiful roses—Chinas and Noisettes mostly, both identified and unknown ones.

Over a period of time, I found many of the Old Noisettes. One was "Fewell's Noisette," which I came across in an old cemetery in upstate South Carolina. It was growing on the grave of a Mr. Fewell, a soldier with a Confederate marker on his grave. The rose looked much like 'Champneys' Pink Cluster', yet it is not quite the same. Today "Fewell's Noisette" is in commerce for all to grow and enjoy, but sadly is no longer to be found in the cemetery.

Mrs. Westwood gave me "Charleston Blush Noisette," one of the loveliest of the 'Blush Noisette'

Above: Old Noisettes at Boone Hall Plantation
Right: 'Blush Noisette' (photos by Malcolm Manners)

types. She had gotten it from her cook, who had received it from another family who had brought it from Charleston many years ago. Another "found" Old Noisette is "Tutta's Mountain Cabin Noisette." A Noisette of simplest form, its dainty blooms are much like 'Champneys' Pink Cluster' but are a little smaller in size. My sister found it growing in the yard of her old stone farmhouse, which was located along the small scenic Highway #11 in the South Carolina foothills of the Blue Ridge Mountains, overlooking Glassy Rock Mountain and ancient apple orchards.

As I collected old roses, I seemed mostly to find roses like "Charleston Blush Noisette" and "Tutta's Mountain Cabin Noisette"—bushes of small, full and fragrant roses growing in clusters. In soft pastel colors of pink, lavender, apricot, and yellow, these types of roses bloomed repeatedly. I found them growing throughout the South in the oldest places, places that had remained undisturbed for many years.

What were these roses? Where did they originally come from? After many months of research and talking with people who grew these kinds of roses, I began to find a few possible answers. On his plantation near Charleston, a man by the name of John Champneys had developed and raised a rose that was eventually named after him. His rose, 'Champneys' Pink Cluster', was found to be a cross between 'Old Blush', a rose from China, and *Rosa moschata*, the ancient 'Musk Rose' that is celebrated in old European literature. Champneys' small pink rose was the first of a new class of roses—roses which eventually became known as the Noisettes.

Found roses like the Old Noisette types that I was discovering throughout South Carolina were typically loved and passed along, sometimes with a name but often with a story. The oral history of a particular rose may be the only information we will ever have as to its origin. Take, for example, the story of Daisy Norton Crouch and her musk rose, which was told to her daughter Perrine Crouch, who in turn passed it along to me. As a young bride, Daisy brought a

cutting of the old 'Musk Rose', *R. moschata* from the small South Carolina town of Islandton to Saluda, South Carolina in the early 1900s. Islandton is only 35 miles from where John Champneys' plantation was located. This is important because Islandton is the nearest to Charleston that we have a record of an old planting of *R. moschata,* one of the parents of 'Champneys' Pink Cluster', which is the first Noisette.

Daisy Norton Crouch's story underscores why it is so important that we record all that we find about each unidentified foundling rose. Every scrap of information adds to the Noisette story. And nothing is quite like the excitement of sharing the news of a found old rose, wrapping tiny cuttings to mail to a fellow collector, or watching as tiny rose leaves sprout and unfold and grow on a rooted cutting. These roses and the people who found them not only become a part of history, but they also become an integral part of our lives.

Living as I do near Charleston, I began to realize how important this fascinating class of roses was to the city's history. At every opportunity, I endeavored to introduce these lovely old roses and to encourage people to plant them in their own gardens. I began to share rooted cuttings and plants of these roses in my sales booth at garden festivals. People who lived in Charleston and nearby communities eagerly took them home. They were interested! I became increas-

ingly aware of the importance of teaching others the story of these forgotten roses.

Eventually an opportunity arose to invite the International Heritage Rose Conference, which convenes somewhere in the world approximately every two years, to come to Charleston. An interested group of Charlestonians formed a committee and began planning the 9th International Heritage Rose Conference to be held in Charleston, South Carolina in October of 2001. The focus of the conference was the Noisettes, this wonderful class of roses whose birthplace was Charleston. And out of our plans for the conference grew the Heritage Rose Trail, which winds through Charleston, and a study garden planted with of all of the earliest true Noisettes that we could obtain.

Thankfully, the Old Noisettes are still among us after nearly two hundred years—some passed down in families, some planted on a loved one's grave as was the custom in earlier times. Many still thrive undisturbed in older gardens, still blooming season by season even though their names are unknown. These are our Old Noisettes. How exciting and rewarding it has been to discover these beautiful, historic treasures in our own backyards and to give them their honored place in the world of roses today. ✍

Catalogue of the Old Noisettes

Gregg Lowery

THE SUBTLE VARIATIONS found in the Old Noisettes, the 'Champneys' Pink Cluster' types, may not excite a modern rose grower accustomed to large flowers in a palette of vivid hues. But to lovers of old things, gardeners touched by demure flowers that bespeak an earlier life in America, these Noisettes are treasured heirlooms.

This guide to the Old Noisettes offers a glimpse of their fragile beauty. To aid the gardener in understanding each variety and attempting to select among them, it includes observations on their flower size and color as well as their habits of growth and bloom. Also noted are the date that each cultivar was introduced, and the breeder or nursery that introduced it.

Many of the Old Noisettes grown today were rediscovered in cemeteries and churchyards, old home-

sites and roadsides. Having lost the original names under which they were introduced, they are known under the "mystery names" given to them by those who found them. The provenance provided may be the name of the finder or the nursery that reintroduced it, and where it was found. Roses known as foundling roses represent unsolved mysteries and are grouped and listed separately. Old rose lovers around the world continue to study these varieties, so one day their original names may come to light.

The Old Noisettes continue to inspire rose growers with their fragrance, grace, and abundance. It is little wonder that a number of new seedlings have been bred in recent years. These include 'Miss Ruth', a seedling discovered in my garden, which honors the Noisette champion Ruth Knopf; 'June Anne', raised by amateur breeder Robert Rippetoe of Palm Springs, California; and 'Sarasota Spice', raised by John Starnes of Tampa, Florida. With these seedlings of the Old Noisettes and with lost cultivars waiting to be rediscovered, future catalogues will surely expand, and the preservation of a beautiful, historic group of old roses will be ensured.

Previous page: 'Multiflore de Vaumarcus'
(photo by Étienne Bouret)
Above: 'Aimée Vibert' (photo by Gregg Lowery)

Aimée Vibert

Introduced in France, 1828 by Jean-Pierre Vibert

With very double, porcelain-white flowers of globular form, each two inches across, 'Aimée Vibert' has broad clusters of twenty or so blooms, which appear continually through the seasons. The plant is quite dwarf, reaching 2 feet or so, with bushy growth and fresh green leaves. Its scent, which is held within the blooms, is musky and sweet.

Aimée Vibert Scandens

Climbing sport of Aimée Vibert, introduced in England, 1841 by William Curtis

Widely grown and loved, this climbing sport of 'Aimée Vibert' sends out arching canes of 6 to 7 feet long, making an excellent small climber. The pale green foliage contrasts with the rich greens of other roses. Like some other climbing sports of bush roses, this sometimes does not rebloom after early summer. Pearl-white flowers are identical to those of the sport parent.

Belle Vichyssoise

Introduced as 'Cornélie' in France, 1858 by Moreau-Robert; collected at Vichy, France, 1895 and reintroduced by Lévêque

One-inch blooms of blush pink in very large clusters are very reminiscent of the flowers of 'Blush Noisette', with which it has been confused. The Hampton Park Noisette Study has shown that the two roses are not identical. A bushy grower to 6 feet or more, it produces a magnificent display of blooms that truly rival those of 'Blush Noisette'.

Blush Noisette

Introduced in the USA, 1817 by Philippe Noisette

Portrayed by Pierre-Joseph Redouté in his famous gallery of roses from Josephine Bonaparte's garden, Malmaison,

'Blush Noisette' improved on its parent, 'Champneys' Pink Cluster', with dense bunches of globular flowers, well-petaled and blushed with rose pink. The blooms are 2 inches across and come in heads of 30 or more buds. The perfume is musky and soft, as perfect as the Damask scent. As a shrub it is stout, reaching 7 feet in good sunny conditions and climbing to 12 feet in shade.

Bougainville

Introduced in France, 1822 by Pierre Cochet *père* and Jean-Pierre Vibert

More broad spreading than most Noisettes, 'Bougainville' (or 'Bouganville'), is named for a French naval officer, Admiral Bouganville. It has the character of a Hybrid Musk rose or of a large Polyantha and produces large, domed clusters of half-inch blooms of deep rose pink, rose red in the bud. The petals are rolled and pointed in a spiky frill in the open flowers.

Bouquet Tout Fait

Introduced in France, before 1836 by Jean Lafay

The perfectly formed flowers of 'Bouquet Tout Fait' often reach 3 inches across, full of petals of white with a cream blush. They appear in large clusters on a robust plant of 6 feet or more. In autumn this prolific bloomer delights gardeners with its massive clusters of bloom arising from new stems from the base. It is richly scented, with a musky, peppery aroma.

Camélia Rose

Introduced in France, before 1830 by Nicolas-Joseph Prévost *fils*

Wiry of growth, with a wispy casual habit, 'Camélia Rose' nods its rounded blooms in a graceful way, dripping small lilac-pink clusters. This rose may have some Tea rose in its heritage or perhaps an added layer of China rose. The flowers, which reach 2 inches across, are cupped like 'Old Blush', and the plant, an arching 6-foot fountain with slender leaves, appears transparent at times.

Top: 'Bougainville'
Above: 'Bouquet Tout Fait' (photos by Gregg Lowery)

Top: 'Camélia Rose'
Above: 'Fellemberg' (photos by Gregg Lowery)

Caroline Marniesse

Introduced in France, 1848 by Roeser

Another short-growing Noisette, 'Caroline Marniesse' offers quite double blooms, an inch or so wide, in large, broad clusters, white with a touch of cherry in the bud form. Its habit is spreading, with canes that often grow sideways and sometimes upward, which makes the rose suitable for training against low walls or fences. With a spread of 3 or 4 feet, it serves well as a dwarf, ground-covering plant. The fragrance blends musk with a fruity undertone.

Champneys' Pink Cluster

Introduced in the USA, circa 1802 by John Champneys

Raised by John Champneys, the original and first Noisette is a free-spirited rose that never seems to quit flowering. Cupped blossoms open loose and lightly double, and are white blushed deeply with rose pink. They are small, just an inch or so across, but appear in large pyramidal trusses, arching and elegant on a 6-foot-tall plant that can reach 10 feet in shady conditions. Its fragrance is a sweet version of the perfume of the 'Musk Rose'.

Deschamps

Introduced in France, 1877 by Deschamps

Included in the observational part of the Hampton Park Noisette Study because it has been classed as an Old Noisette by some modern authors, 'Deschamps' differs significantly from this type and should really be grouped with the Tea-Noisettes, which were derived from the Champneys' type. Flowers are vivid cherry-pink to rose pink feathering to near white at the petal bases. The blooms can measure 3 inches across. It is an angling grower, good as a climber.

Fellemberg

Introduced in France, 1834 by Fellemberg

Often sold under the spelling 'Fellenberg', this Noisette appears to have an extra dose of China rose, perhaps through

Top: 'Jacques Amiot'
Above: 'Mary Washington' (photos by Gregg Lowery)

a red China parent like 'Slater's Crimson China'. Flowers are cherry rose with white petal bases, about an inch and a half across, and are produced in large clusters on a vigorous, domed plant of about 5 by 5 feet.

Jacques Amiot

Introduced in France, before 1867 by Varangot

Little information survives from the nineteenth century about this charming rose. Author and rose historian Brent Dickerson shared the small entry from a catalogue by Soupert et Notting Nursery in Luxembourg, which provided a correct spelling, a date, and an introducer. Rather double 3-inch flowers shaped in the flat, almost quartered style of a Gallica rose are rich rose pink, stained deeper at the petal tips, with creamy petal bases. The plant is arching to 5 feet or so across, but only a few feet tall. Fruity perfume seems to indicate a Tea rose parent.

Mary Washington

Found in Virginia, USA, at Mount Vernon, George Washington's estate, circa 1891

An apocryphal story suggests that this rose was raised by George Washington and named for his mother. The plant however did not surface at Mount Vernon until the end of the nineteenth century, and Washington died five years before John Champneys introduced his 'Pink Cluster'. Regardless, it is a very beautiful example of the class, having small, very double blooms less than an inch across, which appear in large, full clusters. The plant grows upright to 5 feet and is stiffly spreading to about 4 feet. It makes a tidy and thrifty shrub that is always in bloom.

Multiflore de Vaumarcus

Introduced in France, circa 1875 by Menet

Cupped, pale blush flowers open to rather perfectly formed rosette flowers that are tinted a rich shade of lilac pink before they fade again to near-white. A very late Old Noisette,

Top: 'Narrow Water'
Above: 'Nastarana' (photos by Gregg Lowery)

'Multiflore de Vaumarcus' is surprisingly simple and antique in style. With an arching habit, it reaches 6 feet or more in height. Its foliage is most distinctive—lustrous, even glossy, and pale lettuce green. Its face powder fragrance is a memory scent, like the perfume of lilacs.

Narrow Water

Sport of Nastarana, introduced in Ireland, circa 1883 by the Daisy Hill Nursery

This rose pink sport of 'Nastarana' differs from its parent in the rich lavender-rose blush of the semidouble flowers, which form perfect little saucers 1 to 2 inches in width. Nearly single but holding a few smaller petaloides near the stamens, the flowers have a strong scent—the hallmark of 'Nastarana', which is widely considered one of the most fragrant of roses. The plant, with great elegance and fullness, grows upright to 5 feet and is slightly arching.

Nastarana

Introduced from Persia (Iran), before 1879

Milky cream blossoms of luminous quality set 'Nastarana' apart from the other old named cultivars. It is in every other way identical to its sport 'Narrow Water'. What is most intriguing is the mystery of its origin. It is believed to have come from Persia in the nineteenth century, but this may be a case of mistaken identity because the original rose of this name, 'Nastaran', should be a large-growing rose with five petals and a unique method of producing flower shoots that continue to elongate and bloom repeatedly. Belgian botanist Ivan Louette revealed in his research that this rose was brought to France at the end of the nineteenth century, but it does not appear to exist today in Europe or America. Somehow, perhaps because of the fame of the great fragrance of 'Nastaran', the Persian rose, its name was transferred to a Noisette rose. This rose should perhaps be counted among the "mystery" Noisettes.

Above: 'Princesse de Nassau' (photo by Gregg Lowery)

Princesse de Nassau

Introduced in France, 1835 by Jean Laffay

Perhaps the most exciting of the named Noisettes, 'Princesse de Nassau' is also known as *Rosa moschata autumnalis,* the name under which it came to Graham Stuart Thomas, the British authority on old roses. 'Princesse de Nassau' displays more of the 'Musk Rose' than perhaps any of the others. Tall and arching of habit, with very pale green foliage that stands out in any garden, it begins its display late in the season, like *R. moschata.* The flowers are just an inch wide and are white tinted with creamy yellow. They appear in clusters of fifty or more, and are very fragrant. Once the flowering begins it does not cease until winter; the branches bow low with the weight of thousands of trusses of bloom. The rose can reach 8 feet in the open with a spread of 12 feet, and in the shade it rushes upward to scramble into tree limbs if it can.

FOUNDLING OR MYSTERY CULTIVARS

Bermuda Kathleen

Found in Bermuda in the garden of Mrs. Hilda Horsfield, circa 1956

Simple, 2-inch flowers of five petals begin cream and blush pink then deepen to rosy-lilac tinted with red. The panicles of bloom are broad; they rain over the tall, upright shrub, collapsing the branches and creating a mound of great beauty. Its discovery in the garden of Mrs. Hilda Horsfield in the 1950s on the island of Bermuda is recounted in the delightful 1997 book *Roses in Bermuda.* Once believed to be the Hybrid Musk rose 'Kathleen', "Bermuda Kathleen" appears to be related to the old China rose 'Mutabilis'. It displays the color mutations so unique to that old mystery rose.

Cato's Cluster

Found in Virginia, USA, by Carl Cato

Old rose collector Carl Cato of Virginia discovered this beauty in a Virginia garden. For some years he suspected it to be the original 'Champneys' Pink Cluster'. The genetic research performed at Florida Southern College on behalf of the Noisette Study Garden in Charleston, South Carolina, has shown that this rose differs from a number of roses that have been thought to be John Champneys' rose. "Cato's Cluster" makes trusses of 2-inch blooms, rose pink to blush pink, semidouble and very fragrant. Very much in the style of 'Blush Noisette', the plant is upright and arching; it reaches about 5 feet in the open.

Fewell's Noisette

Found in South Carolina, USA, by Ruth Knopf

Discovered by Ruth Knopf in a cemetery in Rock Hill, South Carolina, "Fewell's Noisette" is a very dense grower with upright canes and dense panicles of bloom. The clean white,

1-inch flowers are barely touched with pink, neat and small, rounded in outline with a tidy form, softened by a few central petaloides that curl inward. The petals are long and pointed, making a charming packet of ribbons tied in a bow. The plant is compact and stays to about 4 feet in full sun.

Frazer's Pink Musk

Found in South Carolina, USA, and displayed at
The Huntington Botanical Gardens, circa 1980

While this may yet prove to be identical with the Noisette called "Lingo Musk," the genetic study seems to indicate that the two are not identical. In the 1980s this rose grew in The Huntington Botanical Gardens, and was believed to be the rose raised by the Charleston botanist and nurseryman John Frazer, a contemporary of Philippe Noisette and John Champneys. This tall, broad plant can send up canes of 7 to 8 feet in late summer and autumn, each of which finishes in a great panicle of flowers. The blooms are small, an inch or so across, rosy pink to blush, with a sweet, musky scent.

Haynesville Pink Cluster

Found in Louisiana, USA by Tommy Adams in 1988

Small flowered with loosely double blooms in airy clusters, "Haynesville Pink Cluster" makes a great arching mound and is more truly climbing in nature than most of the Champneys' types. The open blooms are an inch or less across, and the plant can achieve 10 feet or more in height and breadth. In Sebastopol, California, it is always in bloom. In a cool summer climate, it is very susceptible to powdery mildew. Perhaps one of the Noisettes that is most tolerant of shade, it will bloom as abundantly in shade as in full sun. Tommy Adams discovered this rose in Haynesville, Louisiana, while working for The Antique Rose Emporium, which reintroduced it in the late 1980s.

Top: "Frazer's Pink Musk"
Above: "Haynesville Pink Cluster" (photos by Gregg Lowery)

La Nymphe

Found in California, USA, by Fred Boutin, circa 1985

The name given this foundling refers to a Tea-Noisette rose descended from 'Maréchal Niel', and the attribution is incorrect. Nonetheless, despite the soft blush coloring of the blooms and the blowsy quality of the flowers and their large open clusters, it is probably the offspring of a Tea rose crossed with an Old Noisette. The 3-inch semidouble flowers are large-petaled, somewhat pointed in the bud, and open cupped. It is a climbing rose that will reach 10 feet tall and wide. The rich, fresh fragrance owes its fruity sweetness to a Tea rose ancestor. Discovered in the Gilliam Cemetery in Sebastopol, California, by Fred Boutin, "La Nymphe" has been seen surviving in many California waysides.

Lingo Musk

Found in Florida, USA, by Mr. Lingo, distributed in 1970 by Joseph Kern Nursery

With huge clusters of blush pink flowers touched rosy on the petal edges, "Lingo Musk" creates a continuous and generous display of bloom. The plant, which is upright and arching, provided a touchstone for the observational phase of the Hampton Park Noisette Study. Very much the archetype of the Champneys' type, it displays many of the common traits of the Noisettes in this group. One-inch blooms are semidouble, blowsy, and fragrant. The stature of the bush is modest and upright to about 4 or 5 feet. Mr. Lingo of Florida passed his discovery on to the Joseph Kern Nursery in Ohio. Rosarian Léonie Bell ordered it, grew it, and suspected it to be the long lost "Frazer's Pink Musk." It is uncertain whether this plant is distinct from the "Frazer's Pink Musk" that was grown at The Huntington Botanical Gardens; however, the genetic study portion of the Hampton Park Noisette Study seems to indicate that they are different.

Top: "La Nymphe"
Above: "Mrs. Woods' Lavender-Pink Noisette"
(photos by Gregg Lowery)

Top: "Placerville White Noisette"
Above: "St. Leonard" (photos by Gregg Lowery)

Mrs. Woods' Lavender-Pink Noisette

Found in California, USA, by Doris Woods, circa 1985

An elegant, richly colored Noisette with globular blooms of deep lavender-pink, this rose has flowers that are nearly 2 inches across. The plant grows vigorously up and arching to 8 feet or more. It is quite resistant to mildew, even in shade, as evidenced by the success of the mother plant, which was found in the foggy north coastal town of Fort Bragg, California. It grew in the garden of Doris Woods' mother, who passed it on in the 1980s to nurserywoman Joyce Demits of Heritage Rose Gardens. This rose, which is identical to the foundlings "Mt. Vernon Purple" and "Chester Cemetery," may be the old nineteenth-century French cultivar 'La Marseillaise'.

Natchitoches Noisette

Found in Louisiana, USA, by Bill Welch in 1983

In the observational phase of the Hampton Park Noisette Study, this rose struck the observers as truly distinctive: it seemed to differ markedly from the Noisette type. Though the plant is compact and branching like 'Champneys' Pink Cluster', the foliage is lustrous and dark, much closer to that of a China rose. The flowers are small—an inch across, cherry-rose fading to light pink—and reminiscent of the blooms of 'Old Blush China'. "Natchitoches Noisette" forms a broad shrub, 4 feet tall and 5 feet wide, with a clean and glistening appearance. Bill Welch discovered this in an old cemetery in the historic Louisiana town of Natchitoches, and passed it on to The Antique Rose Emporium, which reintroduced it in the 1980s.

Placerville White Noisette

Found in California, USA, by Phillip Robinson, circa 1985

So many rose rustlers in California have collected cuttings from the plant of this rose in the Placerville Cemetery over the years that it has gathered to itself a number of mystery names, including "Zeiss White" and "Jacob Zeiss," in honor of the gravesite on which it grows. A personal favorite, it has pure-white flowers, quite small and double, packed tightly

Above: "Tutta's Mountain Cabin Noisette"
(photo by Gregg Lowery)

into very large clusters. The inch-wide blooms are held close into a dense shrub that grows slowly over time to 5 feet tall and nearly 5 feet wide. At first glimpse it seems to have been clipped over like a ball of boxwood, and that is the beauty of this unforgettable rose.

Secret Garden Noisette

Found in California, USA, by Joyce Demits, circa 1993

Nurserywoman Joyce Demits discovered this white Noisette in California's historic Gold Country in the mining town of Jamestown. Its flowers are particularly fragrant and reminiscent of the fabled musk hybrid 'Nastarana'. A typical Old Noisette in its habit, "Secret Garden Noisette" grows upright to 5 feet and covers itself all summer with broad clusters of 2-inch blooms. The creamy white petals are neatly arranged, pointed, and packed with a formal flair.

St. Leonard

Found in Maryland, USA, in the garden of a friend of Ethelyn Emery Keays by Rev. Douglas T. Seidel, circa 1970

Found over a wide area from Maryland to Ohio and brought to California in the 1970s, this rose was given its mystery name by old rose writer Ethelyn Emery Keays, who discovered it at the St. Leonard post office in Maryland. Rev. Douglas Seidel rediscovered "St. Leonard" at the home of a friend of Mrs. Keays after her death. Large, blowsy flowers of near white with bold, ribbon-like petals can measure more than 2 inches wide. They form clusters of broad, drooping flower stalks. The plant is robust, arching and trailing. with deep green foliage. Misidentified as 'Jeanne d'Arc', this rose is still sold as such.

Tutta's Mountain Cabin Noisette

Found in South Carolina, USA, by Tutta Mood, circa 1985

Ruth Knopf's sister Tutta Mood found this growing at a small mountain cabin she purchased in the 1980s in South Carolina. Another rose growing nearby turned out to be a form of 'Blush Noisette', but this plant was unique. Rose pink flowers turn blush with age. Blooming in generous broad clusters, they are small, semidouble and loose. In my Sebastopol, California garden, "Tutta's Mountain Cabin Noisette" is among the most prolific of bloomers. It has a preference for filtered shade, but even the hottest days fail to wilt the delicate petals.

NOTE: *Four roses that were included in the DNA portion of the Hampton Park Noisette Study are now missing from the Noisette Study Garden: "Jim's Fence Corner," "Chester Cemetery," "Mt. Vernon," and "Setzer Noisette." "Jim's Fence Rose" and "Chester Cemetery" were too small to include in the morphological part of the Hampton Park Noisette Study.*

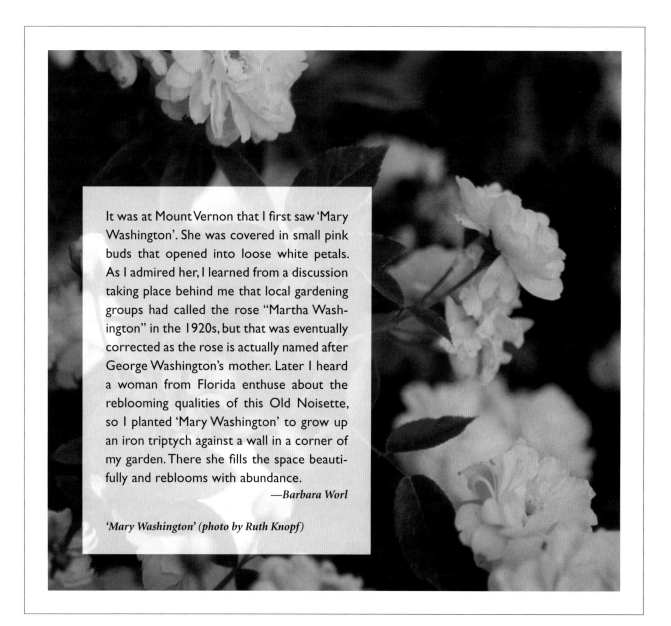

It was at Mount Vernon that I first saw 'Mary Washington'. She was covered in small pink buds that opened into loose white petals. As I admired her, I learned from a discussion taking place behind me that local gardening groups had called the rose "Martha Washington" in the 1920s, but that was eventually corrected as the rose is actually named after George Washington's mother. Later I heard a woman from Florida enthuse about the reblooming qualities of this Old Noisette, so I planted 'Mary Washington' to grow up an iron triptych against a wall in a corner of my garden. There she fills the space beautifully and reblooms with abundance.

—*Barbara Worl*

'Mary Washington' (photo by Ruth Knopf)

CHAPTER SIX

The Hampton Park Noisette Study

Malcolm M. Manners

W HEN ONE TRIES TO IDENTIFY a rose or the differences between two roses, it can be quite confounding. For such comparisons to be valid, it is important that the roses be grown under as nearly identical conditions as possible. To minimize the variation that can occur due to differences in climate, soil type, and day-to-day care by the gardener, Charleston's Hampton Park Noisette Study Garden was to provide such a place for the study of the Noisette roses.

In this large garden, rosarian Ruth Knopf and city horticulturist JoAnn Breland brought together an amazing collection of Noisettes, including many examples of 'Champneys' Pink Cluster', 'Blush Noisette', and other historic roses from a variety of sources, including commercial old rose nurseries and private growers.

Also included were many "found" roses that appeared to fit among the Noisettes.

The goal was to do a comparison study of all these roses. While such a study could never hope to guarantee that "this rose is definitely the original 'Champneys' Pink Cluster' and that rose is not," it should be able to say that the rose grown as 'Champneys' Pink Cluster' by nursery A is the same rose that nurseries B and C grow under that name, and the same as the found rose "Jane Doe" but different from the rose nurseries D and E sell as 'Champneys' Pink Cluster'.

The methods used by the Noisette Study team to study the roses included visual observation in the garden on several occasions as well as DNA analysis, using the RAPD-PCR method. The team who performed the garden observations included Ruth

Previous page: Closeup of 'Blush Noisette' buds
Above: Study team members Gregg Lowery and Phillip Robinson
(photos by Malcolm Manners)
Opposite: "Lingo Musk" (photo by Gregg Lowery)

Knopf, JoAnn Breland, nurseryman Gregg Lowery, rose expert Philip Robinson, and myself. We observed and recorded botanical characteristics such as flower size, petal count, fragrance, prickle description, leaf size and shape, presence or absence of glandular hairs, and hip shape.

Morphological Study

In observing differences among the Noisettes in the Hampton Park Noisette Study Garden, we decided to use the found rose "Lingo Musk" as the example of a "typical" Old Noisette rose. We then compared the other roses in the garden to see how their characteristics differed from the "typical" characteristics of "Lingo Musk."

Armed with this description of the typical Old Noisette, many other rose varieties in the garden were observed for comparison. The table on pages 48–49 is a summary of the differences in the flowers and buds of the varieties we observed. We also looked at the leaves of the plants and noted differences from the "standard" Noisette. Finally, for each we examined and recorded differences in the prickles and in the growth habit of the overall bush. So while all of the roses we studied exhibit many similar characteristics, and while we recognize them all as Noisettes, they do have definite, observable differences.

DNA Analysis

In addition to the visual observations made in the Hampton Park Noisette Study Garden, some of the plants were tested by RAPD-PCR analysis at Florida Southern College, where I teach, by molecular geneticist Dr. Nancy Morvillo and several student researchers. The DNA analyses were conducted over two summers and included several studies. The *Proceedings of the 9th International Conference on Heritage Roses*, which is available from the Heritage Rose Foundation, contains full reports on that research, but here is a summary of the results.

Characteristics of "Lingo Musk"—A Typical Old Noisette

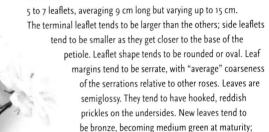

Plants

Bushy, spreading and upright. The inflorescence has bracts, which are glandular and serrate, with somewhat acuminate tips. The inflorescence is a cymose panicle with up to 150 flowers, red, smooth, thornless, perhaps sparsely pubescent but not glandular. The top center flower bud opens first, followed by lower buds.

Flower pedicel

Red, glandular, and fragrant when touched. The receptacle is finely pubescent, narrowly elongate and slightly rounded, light green or slightly bronzed. Flower buds are ovoid, pointed, and elongated, and bright pink. The sepals reflex strongly, are entire to foliated, are finely glandular and entire.

Petals

Up to 3 cm long, variable in shape from cordate to emarginate droplet-shaped; blush pink, fading to white with a yellowish base. Most flowers have about 17 well-developed petals, and about 12 narrower petaloids. Scent is musky and clove-like (emanating from the petals). Flowers are flat, loose, cupped and reflexed, semidouble with central petaloids, often showing some stamens. Pistils are synstylous.

Leaves

5 to 7 leaflets, averaging 9 cm long but varying up to 15 cm. The terminal leaflet tends to be larger than the others; side leaflets tend to be smaller as they get closer to the base of the petiole. Leaflet shape tends to be rounded or oval. Leaf margins tend to be serrate, with "average" coarseness of the serrations relative to other roses. Leaves are semiglossy. They tend to have hooked, reddish prickles on the undersides. New leaves tend to be bronze, becoming medium green at maturity; may be slightly rugose. Petioles usually have some red pigment. The stipules tend to be smooth, but with fine, glossy glands on the edges; they are rather short, very fringed on a large base, and the distal free ends curve back from the petiole. Leaves are somewhat susceptible to black spot disease.

Stems

Tinted red when young, becoming green; glabrous (no hair or fuzz on the surface) with variable internode length up to 5 cm. Tend to be straight (no zig-zag at each node). Prickles are coppery red, maturing to brown, acuminate triangular, 2 to 3 per internode, small to medium in size, randomly spaced along the internode; may be downwardly hooked or straight. When pushed sideways, they snap cleanly from the stem.

STUDY NAME	BUD COLOR	PETAL COLOR	PETAL COUNT	PEDICELS
Lingo Musk (our standard Old Noisette)	bright pink	blush pink, fading white, yellow at base; near-white	17, plus 12 petaloids	red glandular
Placerville White Noisette	blush, some apricot	blush with apricot fading white, yellow base	41, plus 18 petaloids	
La Nymphe	blush to flesh	blush pink	20, plus 10 petaloids (can have more)	
Bougainville	strong mid-pink	clear China pink fading to blush white	35–40	few glands
Mrs. Woods' Lavender-Pink Noisette	deep pink, paling	medium pink fading to pale pink, lavender in tone	25, plus 7 petaloids	few glands
Natchitoches Noisette	similar	creamy white deepening to cherry on outer petals	21, plus 5 petaloids	
Deschamps	red	backs much paler, medium pink with dark pink-toned overlay, especially on veins	50, plus 5 petaloids	
Belle Vichyssoise				
Nastarana	light pink	pale pink fading to white	11, plus 4 petaloids	
Fellenberg	red	deep pink, yellow dot at base	22, plus 8 petaloids	pubescent
Narrow Water	pink	pale pink fading white, white striped underneath	11, plus 8 petaloids	
Aimée Vibert Scandens				
Jim's Fence Corner				
Haynesville Pink Cluster	deep pink, almost red	warm blush, fading white, yellowish base	21, plus 8 petaloids	
Bouquet Tout Fait	white	white with yellow base	20, plus 5 petaloids	
Setzer Noisette	blush white	white, yellow base	30, plus some petaloids	
Mt. Vernon Noisette	white		36, plus 5 petaloids	pubescent
Fewell's Noisette	pale pink	blush to white	17, plus 8 petaloids	
Mary Washington	pale pink to white	flesh blush to white	41, plus 22 petaloids	pubescent
Jeanne d'Arc	creamy white	white, base turning red with age	16, plus 12 petaloids	

RECEPTACLE	LEAVES	TERMINAL LEAFLET SIZE	STIPULES	PRICKLES	PLANT HABIT
pubescent	5-7 leaflets	larger than others		2–3 per internode, straight	bushy, spreading and upright
	smaller			1–2, some hooked	compact
		equal in size		4–5, large	
		equal in size	fringed and red	large	compact
		equal in size			
				few	
		fewer leaflets			
		fewer leaflets			
		rugose		few	large and sprawling
	glandular			few	
	glandular			few	
	glandular	lots of glands		hooked	
				few	
				large	compact

The musk rose (*Rosa moschata* Herrmann) is one of the purported parents of 'Champneys' Pink Cluster', and therefore the ancestor of all the Noisettes. In their three forms (single, double, and the very double "Temple" type), plants from many provenances in the United States and England were compared. They were all virtually identical, leading us to believe that all true musk roses currently being grown are either the same cultivar or simple mutations from a single original plant. That is convenient from the standpoint of studying the Noisettes because instead of having a highly variable species as the ancestor, we have just one candidate for that ancestor.

The other purported parent of 'Champneys' Pink Cluster' is 'Old Blush', a rose still commonly grown and generally accepted as the original cultivar grown under that name. So we tested plants of 'Champneys' Pink Cluster' from several sources (The Antique Rose Emporium, the Center for Historic Plants, Chamblee's Roses, Ruth Knopf, Vintage Gardens, and Wayside Gardens) and plants of a similar rose known as "Cato's Cluster," which is often grown and exhibited as 'Champneys' Pink Cluster', and compared them to each other as well as to 'Old Blush' and the single-flowered 'Musk Rose'.

Left: 'Alister Stella Gray'
Right: "Placerville White Noisette" (photos by Ruth Knopf)

Roses in the Third DNA Study

Found Noisettes
Chester Cemetery*
Fewell's Noisette
Jeanne d'Arc
Jim's Fence Corner*
Lingo Musk
Manchester Guardian Angel
Mrs. Woods' Lavender-Pink Noisette
Mt. Vernon Noisette*
Natchitoches Noisette
Placerville White Noisette
Pleasant Hill Cemetery
Setzer Noisette*
Tutta's Pink Noisette

Named Cultivars
Alister Stella Gray
Belle Vichyssoise
Bougainville
Camélia Rose
Fellemberg
Mary Washington
Narrow Water
Nastarana
Princesse de Nassau

* These are now missing from the Noisette Study Garden.

Above: 'Narrow Water' (photo by Étienne Bouret)

All of the roses marketed as 'Champneys' Pink Cluster' were virtually identical to each other, and approximately half of their DNA bands matched those of 'Old Blush'. The other half matched bands of the 'Musk Rose'. 'Champneys' Pink Cluster' had no DNA bands unaccounted for by one or the other of the parents. These data tell us that the old rose nursery industry in the United States is consistent in its marketing of the same rose, under the name 'Champneys' Pink Cluster', and that that plant is very likely the direct offspring of 'Old Blush' and the 'Musk Rose', which leads us to believe that 'Champneys' Pink Cluster' is the correct identification. The "Cato's Cluster" rose, as expected, appears to be closely related but not genetically identical to those roses grown as 'Champneys' Pink Cluster'.

Several accessions of 'Blush Noisette' (from The Antique Rose Emporium, Ruth Knopf, Rose Guardians, and Vintage Gardens) were also compared to each other as well as to 'Champneys' Pink Cluster'. Again, all of the so-called 'Blush Noisette' accessions appear to be identical, and approximately half of their DNA can be attributed to 'Champneys' Pink Cluster'. These data lead us to believe that the plant currently grown and sold as 'Blush Noisette' is probably identified correctly.

Study of "Found and Known" Noisettes

A third study compared many of the "found" Noisette roses as well as a few other "known" Noisettes in the Hampton Park Garden to each other as well as to 'Champneys' Pink Cluster' and 'Blush Noisette'. The results of these DNA studies were as follows:

1. None of the plants studied was identical to any other in the group.
2. All of the plants studied showed considerable relationship to each other, and shared DNA with 'Champneys' Pink Cluster' and/or 'Blush Noisette'. These findings support the concept that there is a large "hybrid swarm" of Noisettes in the style of 'Champneys' Pink Cluster' in the

Southern United States and that these roses were probably the result of several generations of seedlings, often sown by birds, or were otherwise "accidents" in gardens. The findings show that all of the roses in this study trace their ancestry to 'Champneys' Pink Cluster'. ✍

What is RAPD-PCR?

DNA is the genetic material of a plant, the chemical blueprint containing all the instructions for making it. Some of that DNA is quite similar from plant to plant; some of it will be different among different varieties. All roses share more identical DNA with each other than any rose would share with a magnolia tree or banana plant. Roses within a horticultural class (Noisette, Tea, China) are assumed to share more of their DNA than they would with those of a different class. The entire DNA sequence should be identical in all plants of a particular cultivar.

RAPD-PCR (randomly amplified polymorphic DNA-polymerase chain reaction) is a system in which we chop a plant's DNA into small pieces, and then multiply those pieces to very large numbers so they can be observed. We use "primers," small chunks of purchased DNA, to choose the exact breaking points for the plant's DNA. The primers match up to specific areas along the DNA. A primer usually attachs itself at several points along the DNA strand, so we end up with several small chunks of DNA to work with, in each rose sample, for each primer used.

If two roses of the same variety are tested, the chunks should always be identical for a particular primer. In different roses, the primers may attach at different spots, so the "chunks" will differ between the varieties. In the process for separating chunks, which is called gel electrophoresis, the DNA sample is applied to one end of the gel plate, which looks like a block of gelatin. An electric current is run through the gel and the DNA is forced to migrate down the length of the gel by the electricity. The longer DNA pieces move down the gel much more slowly than the shorter pieces. The ultimate result is that "bands" of DNA appear all along the gel.

If we run RAPD samples of several roses, each will make a characteristic series of bands at very specific places on the gel. The more of those bands that match up to those of another rose, the more closely related those two roses are likely to be. If we're looking at a parent and offspring, the offspring should have approximately half of the bands of the parent. If we have both parents in the study, the offspring should have about half of its bands from each parent, and should have no bands that fail to match either parent.

How can one describe a beautiful rose? How can you convey the joyous sensation evoked by the light green leaves stretched out in the early morning sun, wet with dew and holding up for your admiration pale yellow bunches of crumpled petals, each folded around a dark green eye? And in between, the crimson buds pouting from flaring grey-green sepals, waiting to be kissed? Kiss the bud and breathe the fragrance of the smiling bloom, face to face, cheek to cheek. Savor the fragrance of the soft silk petals and say, 'Céline Forestier'.

—*Gwen Fagan*

'Céline Forestier' in a private garden in South West Australia (photo by Odile Masquelier)

CHAPTER SEVEN

France and the Tea-Noisettes

Odile Masquelier

ACCORDING TO THE FRENCH nurseryman
Louis Noisette, brother of Philippe Noisette,
the first Noisette rose arrived in France in 1814, the
year the Empress Josephine died at Malmaison. Others believe the first Noisette arrived in 1816, 1817 or
even 1818. Whatever the date, 'Blush Noisette' never
arrived in France. The rose that did reach France
goes by several names: 'Noisette Carnée', 'Rose de
Philippe Noisette', or the 'Flesh-colored Noisette
rose'. The name "Noisette" does not come from the
French for hazelnut, but from *noiseux* (*noisy* in English), an old French word that is no longer in use.

In 1820 the renowned French artist Pierre-Joseph Redouté painted the rose, giving it the name
R. noisettiana, or 'Rose de Philippe Noisette'. Three
years later, Nathalie d'Esmenard, one of Redouté's
best pupils, succeeded brilliantly in copying the
painting. Her watercolor on vellum may be found
today at the Fitzwilliam Museum in Cambridge,
England.

In France, this new American rose was classified
as *Rosa noisettiana*, a species, by Bosc, Pronville and
Thory, despite the opposition of various rosarians
who claimed that the new rose was a hybrid. Philippe

Rosa Indica vulgaris.   *Rosier des Indes commu*

Previous page: The rose depicted in this painting by French painter Simon St. Jean could be the Tea-Noisette 'Chromatella'.
Oil on canvas (private collection)
Above: Rosa indica *by Pierre-Joseph Redouté*
Right: 'Aimée Vibert' (photo by Étienne Bouret)

Noisette himself stated this in a letter to his brother Louis. French botanists Pierre Boitard in 1836 and Jean-Louis Auguste Loiseleur-Deslongchamps in 1844 strongly protested the classification of this new rose as a species. They believed the flesh-colored Noisette to be nothing more than a *R. moschata* hybrid and that it should be called 'Hybrid of Noisette'.

There are many cultivars of the flesh-colored Noisette, and they do not all bear the same name. Narcisse Desportes calls it *R. noisettiana vulgaris.* Lyon botanist Nicolas-Charles Seringe calls the rose *R. indica noisettiana.* In Geneva, Switzerland, the rose is known as *R. paniculata.* For England's Mrs. Catherine Gore, author of *The Rose Fancier's Manual* (1838), it is the 'Flesh-colored Noisette', and for nurseryman Thomas Smith of Newry, Northern Ireland, 'Blush Cluster'. In the French countryside people simply call the rose 'La Belle Noisette' or 'La Bengale Noisette'. Despite these variations, everyone did agree that the rose should bear the name "Noisette." Strangely, not one of them—neither Auguste de Pronville in 1824, Louis Noisette in his 1825 catalogue, Narcisse Desportes in 1828, Alfred Deseglise, nor master rose hybridizer Jean-Pierre Vibert in 1828—mentions John Champneys and 'Champneys' Pink Cluster'.

Meanwhile, mindful of his jewel, Louis Noisette jealously kept the 'Flesh-colored Noisette' and hybridized it. He probably did not know that two rooted cuttings of it had been sent to Jacques Durand, a nurseryman in Rouen, Normandy, and that Durand propagated it and freely sold it around. Alexandre Hardy, curator at the Luxembourg garden of the largest rose collection since the disappearance of Empress Josephine's at Malmaison, had also received a specimen of *R. noisettiana*. Charles Durand is also reported to have received a seed packet from Columbia, South Carolina, from which came the 'Yellow-hearted Noisette', ('Noisette à coeur jaune') a rose with a sulphur-colored center. Durand was a big exporter of roses across the Channel, so doubtless this is how the 'Yellow-hearted Noisette' found its way to England. It may even be the origin of 'Smithii Yellow Noisette', a rose that is supposedly extinct.

Only ten years after the Noisette rose's introduction in France, the French horticulturists were marketing 102 Noisette varieties. Horticulturists and florists described them as hardy roses with large clusters of flowers, blooming successively from June to November. Louis Noisette lists 35 Noisettes in his catalogue, while Jean-Pierre Vibert in Chenevières sur Marne offers 85 in his 1828 catalogue. Vibert's collection is the most extensive, with the greatest variety of seedlings, according to M. de Pronville, and gardeners and amateurs alike flocked to Chenevières each year for the roses.

Vibert and Jules Laffay became the main hybridiz-

ers, and were later joined by Victor Verdier. The names they gave the roses they bred are simple: 'Noisette à grandes fleurs', (large-flowered Noisette), 'Noisette à fleurs doubles' (double-flowered Noisette), 'Noisette sarmenteuse' (Rambling Noisette), 'Noisette angevine', 'Noisette pourpre' (Purple Noisette), 'Noisette Jacques', 'A Fleurs Roses' (pink-flowered Noisette), 'Pourpre', and 'Cupidon'.

Everyone began planting the famed 'Aimée Vibert', a shrub Noisette introduced by Vibert in 1828. Also known as 'Bouquet de la Mariée' (Bride's Bouquet), the climbing form was later obtained by Henry Curtis thirteen years later in 1841. And only twenty years after the arrival of 'Noisette Carnée', the *Revue Horticole* reports the availability of five hundred Noisettes.

The Tea-Noisette Roses

In his 1848 edition of *The Rose Garden*, William Paul makes this observation:

The original Noisette was obtained by M. Philippe Noisette, in North America, and sent to Paris in 1817. The peculiar features to notice were its hardy nature, free growth and large clusters of flowers produced very late in the year. Hybridizing with the Tea scented roses extends the range and improves the delicacy of colors, but we are rendering a hardy group of roses tender; this is a matter of regret.

How right was he? In my opinion, the Tea-Noisettes are not only healthy and easy-growing, but include some of the best repeat-flowering and climbing roses.

As soon as 'Parks' Yellow Tea-scented China' was introduced in France in 1825 by Alexander Hardy, then curator of the Luxembourg Garden, both professionals and amateurs began hybridizing it with the Noisette. However, the famous rose that arrived in England with John Parks in 1824 is definitely not the one we have under this name in our gardens today. 'Parks' Yellow' was a repeat-flowering shrub, the yellow counterpart of 'Hume's Blush'. According to Pirolle in the Redouté 1825 Edition, it bore "flow-ers 5–7, 5cms in diameter, petals yellow ochre outside, sulphur yellow within, soon fading to sulphury white after expansion, although in the cool of autumn the initial color is held better." In any case, the rose was a real yellow, vivid enough to be able to produce the yellow Tea-Noisette, and in size, a shrub small enough, according to Thomas Rivers, that it could be sold potted and in full bloom in the fall Parisian flower markets.

Five years later in 1830, two famous Tea-Noisettes appear: 'Jaune Desprez' and 'Lamarque'. Both are a cross between 'Blush Noisette' and 'Parks' Yellow Tea-scented China' and both are still very popular today. More buff cream and pink than yellow, 'Jaune Desprez' (also called 'Desprez à Fleurs Jaunes') is a cold-tolerant, very vigorous, profuse, nonstop bloomer with a delightfully fruity scent. It is also heat and drought-tolerant. I have seen four 'Jaune Desprez' sheltering a terrace in Tuscany on a large pergola 20 feet (6 meters) high and 33 feet (10 meters) long. In the evening the sight and fragrance of thousands of peachy pink blooms were unbelievable.

This rose was nicknamed the "three thousand francs rose." Jean Desprez, who was a famous amateur breeder in Yèbles, could never agree to sell his roses. One day, a Dutch horticulturist, Sisley Van Daël, was so insistent about buying 'Jaune Desprez' that to get it over with, Desprez said, "Look, I just received my new

Left:'Jaune Desprez' (photo by Odile Masquelier)

hothouse's invoice: settle the bill and the rose is yours." The amount was 3,000 francs, a considerable sum, which Van Daël paid on the spot. Hippolyte Jamain also reports that in his final illness Desprez asked for his favorite rose. He feasted his eyes upon it for the last time and then peacefully passed away.

The history of 'Lamarque' is quite different. It was born in a pot in the window box of an amateur, M. Maréchal, a shoemaker in Angers. First named 'Thé Maréchal' (Tea Maréchal), it was then baptized 'Lamarque' after a very faithful general of Napoleon's. 'Lamarque' definitely needs a sunny, sheltered wall to be happy and to display his superb, large, milky white blooms. The rose repeats well and is generous with its blooms until the frost, but is happier without frost. The most spectacular ones I have seen were in private gardens in Northern California and in Western Australia.

In 1832 another amateur, a Lieutenant Colonel Toullier, a former officer of Napoleon's who lived close to Chateau Malmaison, introduced 'La Biche', or 'The Doe'. Very scarce today, 'La Biche' is a lovely small climber. A creamy buff repeating rose, it must have been quite popular as it is often mentioned and illustrated with chromolithographs in rose books of the time (*The Beauties of the Rose* by Henry Curtis, 1850–1853, *Choix des plus belles roses* by Martin Victor Paquet, 1854, and *Les roses* by H. Jamain & E. Forney, 1873).

Left: The Tea-Noisette 'Lamarque'. A detail from La Belle Jardinière *by Simon St. Jean, 1837. Oil on canvas (courtesy of Le Musée des Beaux Arts de Lyon)*
Above left: 'Lamarque'
Above right: 'Gloire de Dijon' (photos by Odile Masquelier)

Then in 1842 came the cherished 'Céline Forestier', a lovely quartered rose of an acid yellow. According to Graham Thomas, it is a gem, but to be truthful a sometimes temperamental one if not located in the right setting. A climber or a large shrub, 'Céline Forestier' is happy scrambling through a small tree, facing south. Its breeder, Victor Trouillard, lived in Angers in the province of Anjou, which for its climate and *art de vivre* was, and still is, the sweetest part of France.

In 1848, Toullier wrote, "'Chromatella', 'Solfatare', 'Lamarque', are these roses more beautiful than the old Noisette? Certainly not, but we are living in times where novelty is a must always and everywhere." This sounds familiar to me. However, these Tea-Noisettes have proved with time to be great additions to our patrimony of roses. From Angers came 'Chromatella' ('Cloth of Gold') bred by Coquereau, and 'Solfatare', bred by Boyau. Both roses, born in 1843, were sulphur-yellow. Coquereau actually lived in the Angers district called La Maître-École. (La Maître-École was, since the 15th century, a famous horticultural school, the most important one in Anjou, and probably in France.) At my home, La Bonne Maison, 'Chromatella' stretches 33 feet (10 meters) against a brick wall. It is an extremely vigorous climber with vanilla cream blooms suffused

Above: A detail from Roses *by nineteenth-century French painter André Perrachon. The author believes the roses may be Noisettes and Tea-Noisettes. Oil on canvas (private collection)*
Right: Two views of 'Maréchal Niel' (photos by Odile Masquelier)

with pink and irregularly edged with carmine. Both it and 'Solfatare' are illustrated by superb chromo-lithographs in *The Rose* by S.B. Parsons, 1847, and in *The Beauties of the Rose* by Henry Curtis, 1850–1853.

'Gloire de Dijon', introduced in 1853, is sometimes considered a Tea, a Noisette, or a Bourbon. Follow-

ing the opinion of Wernt and Hedi Grimm and Gregg Lowery, I include it here. A great rose, it repeats well in the fall, with larger blooms than one of its supposed parents, 'Jaune Desprez'. Sadly the 'Gloire de Dijon' we grow now has lost its vigor, a result perhaps of its one hundred and fifty years of success. At present I am trying to obtain bud wood from an ancient shrub adorning a Victorian mansion in Meursault, France.

'Maréchal Niel', bred by Henri Pradel, a horticulturist in Montauban, is a well-known yellow Tea-Noisette, but its history is perhaps not so well known. In 1857, Pradel was planting some 'Chromatella' roses

for a customer and came up short of a shrub. He replaced it with one of his own seedlings. That same year Victor Verdier was a member of the jury in the Montauban Rose Trial. He noticed the rose and later grafted it. Seven years later, 1864 Verdier introduced and dedicated it to Mme la Maréchale Niel. In the nick of time, someone informed him that Maréchal Niel was a bachelor! I planted 'Maréchal Niel' inside my greenhouse so that I could have roses to look at in March when I am busy tending the early cuttings and seedlings. The old greenhouse is not heated but faces south. I located 'Maréchal Niel' in a corner and trained it on two walls where it opens perfect blooms early in March and then continues blooming for over two months (illustrated in *Les roses* by H. Jamain & E. Forney, 1873, and in *The Rose Garden* by William Paul, 4th Edition 1875).

'Ornement des Bosquets' with its fresh pink to deep pink blooms is not really a Tea-Noisette but a real climber, and a very free and nonstop bloomer. Vigorous, it was introduced by the Parisian merchant Ferdinand Jamin in 1860. Cultivated in Lyon's Botanical Garden, in the Parc de la Tête d'Or, and at L'Haÿ les Roses, it has sadly disappeared from the catalogues and is sometimes mistakenly classified as a Boursault rose. 'Deschamps' a cerise pink Noisette introduced by Deschamps in 1877, is a good companion for 'Ornement des Bosquets'. 'Deschamps' has medium loose flowers in clusters surrounded by lush dark green foliage and repeats with great generosity. Smaller than 'Ornement des Bosquets', it will only reach 10 feet (3 meters).

These two Parisian Noisettes are worthy of a place in any garden. 'Elie Beauvillain' is a late Tea-Noisette, introduced in 1888 from southern France. A small but sturdy climber with large fresh pink blooms, darker coppery pink in the center, she is superb in warm countries where she flowers continuously. 'Marie Dermar', a hybrid of 'Louise d'Arzens', was introduced by Rudolph Geschwind in 1889. Easy to groom, it is the last Noisette to open its fleshy pink blossoms and is a real *bijou*. The perfectly rounded blooms turn pure white at the opening up of the corollas, and the foliage is a healthy dark green. Repeating well, 'Marie Dermar' will easily reach 13 feet (4 meters) on an arch.

Above: 'Deschamps'
Top right: 'Park's Yellow Tea-scented China'
Bottom right: 'Marie Dermar' (photos by Odile Masquelier)

The pseudo 'Parks' Yellow Tea-scented China' is obviously an outstanding, vigorous, nonrepeating rambling Tea and, as Charles Quest-Ritson says, most probably a Tea-Noisette in search of a name. Why not? 'Parks' Yellow' with its large, creamy blooms is the very first large-flowered climber to flourish whatever the weather, and is endowed with a delicate and unforgettable lemony fragrance. It's a must in every garden, whatever its ancestry.

Noisettes of Lyon

The first Noisette born in Lyon is the famous 'Mme Plantier'. Introduced by Plantier in 1835, this rose is sometimes considered an Alba but is best viewed as a nonrecurrent early Noisette. The most glorious 'Mme Plantier' I have ever seen was draped over a wall, glistening in half-shade, at one of the entrances to Nymans Garden in Sussex, England.

One of the best Tea-Noisettes is 'Rêve d'Or'. Bred by Claude Ducher in 1867, 'Rêve d'Or' is not delicate but will bloom more generously if trained on a sunny wall. It offers large buff-yellow roses that display a coppery pink heart. Trained upon a brick wall at La Bonne Maison, it repeats until the frost, with blooms of a stronger yellow in the fall (illustrated in *The Roses* by William Paul, 10th edition).

Five years later in 1872, Claude Ducher introduced 'Bouquet d'Or'. Less vigorous than 'Rêve d'Or', it is similar looking, of a pure yellow, not quite as coppery, and turns out to be the perfect small pillar rose.

'William Allen Richardson' appeared in 1878. It is a sport of 'Rêve d'Or', and was introduced by Claude Ducher's widow and dedicated to a South Carolina citizen who crossed the Atlantic Ocean to choose a rose. Shapeless it may be, as Graham Thomas says, but it is a profuse bloomer if kept lightly pruned and well cleaned after the first flush. It will repeat generously in summer and fall and combines well

Left: 'William Allen Richardson' in Odile's garden, La Bonne Maison
Above: 'Duchesse d'Auerstaedt' (photos by Odile Masquelier)

with 'Crépuscule' (illustrated in *Les plus belles roses au début du 20ème siècle*).

In 1872 'Mme Alfred Carrière', bred by Joseph Schwartz and dedicated to the wife of a keen rose fancier from the Dauphiné, makes its famed debut. This rose has enjoyed a glorious career that time has not diminished. Sturdy, it quickly takes up more than its allotted space and is always the first and last rose to bloom. Trained on a wall or grown as a large shrub,

Above: 'Crépuscule' in early May at La Bonne Maison
Right: 'Rêve d'Or' at La Bonne Maison
(photos by Odile Masquelier)

the soft *rose carné* blooms have a delicate fruity fragrance, which is curiously more intense in the fall.

'Duchesse d' Auerstaëdt' (Bernaix, 1888), perhaps more Tea than Noisette, has the largest roses. The perfectly quartered blooms of an intense golden yellow are endowed with a light tea perfume. Dedicated to a descendant of Maréchal Davoût, Duke of Auerstaëdt, another famous officer of Napoleon's, it generously repeats in summer and fall, enhanced by the deep purple of its new growth.

'Claire Jacquier' (Bernaix, 1888), on the contrary, does not repeat. Although sometimes classified as a Multiflora, it has a creamy yellow Noisette coloring with a coppery pink heart and a fruity scent. Amazingly robust, it can spread within two years over a big arch and is a wonderful sight when in full bloom. While a once-bloomer, it is often mistaken for 'Alister Stella Gray'.

From Jean Pernet, known as Pernet *père*, came 'Triomphe des Noisette', an 1887 seedling of 'Général Jacqueminot', a rather rare Noisette. Its large flowers are of a stunningly bright crimson-pink. They turn raspberry-pink when fully open. An atypical Noisette, it is certainly the darkest of all and one of the largest. Vigorous, it repeats well and has a sweet fragrance.

'Crépuscule', introduced in 1904, may be the most spectacular Tea-Noisette. Its orange-ocher blooms stand out against coppery foliage and repeat generously until the frost, and its colors are luminous in any kind of weather. Its blooms are as intense and brilliant in Southwest Australia as in Cavriglia, Tuscany, or at Mottisfont Abbey in England. The breeder, Francis Dubreuil, was the grandfather of Francis Meilland, who was the breeder of the famous rose 'Peace' ('Mme Antoine Meilland').

My very last Noisette, 'Marguerite Desrayaux', was introduced by Clement and Paul Nabonnand in 1906. It is a flesh-pink Tea-Noisette, a small climber with large roses. An impressive seedling of 'Mme Alfred Carrière', this Noisette is happy in dry weather.

The bulky white chimney against the bright blue sky has been robbed of its glory by a small buff rose. Multiple trusses of the small buff rose are piled one above the other in a golden spire, falling one below the other to the mound at its base where the bright sun has pinned it in a fluttering mass. And when the flowers are fallen and you sigh at the loss, the sun will soon draw trusses for another show. Yellow, buff, and apricot will catch the sun again, for 'Crépuscule' is willing and anxious to please and will shake out tiers of blossoms with the greatest of ease.

—*Gwen Fagan*

Top: 'Crépuscule'
Left: Chimney overgrown with 'Crépuscule' at Salomonsvlei, a farm in South Africa (photos by Gwen Fagan)

CHAPTER EIGHT

The Noisette Study Garden at Hampton Park

JoAnn Breland

CHARLESTON'S HAMPTON PARK, which was named in honor of General Wade Hampton for services rendered to South Carolina, has been a city park since 1903. The area where it is located has a rich and varied history and according to property records, was part of a 190-acre tract deeded to Patrick Scott in 1701. By the time the next deed was recorded, the property had become the 232-acre plantation of John Gibbes. Gibbes is reputed to have had a passion for gardens, but his was destroyed during the Revolutionary War. When the war ended, Charleston's population surged and the plantation was divided into large parcels of land known as the Grove Plantation, which later became the Village of Washington. One of the first large parcels, a 55-acre lot intended to be the Washington Race course, was sold to the Charleston Jockey Club. The Jockey Club went out of business in 1900 and the property went to the Charleston Library Society.

To boost a sagging local economy and to promote Charleston as a major port, the city council and some influential Charlestonians organized the South Carolina Interstate and West Indian Exposition on the property in 1901. In 1906 the city hired the Olmsted Brothers, a Boston-based architectural firm, to create a master plan for a park on the then 130-acre property. Although drives and walkways were laid out according to the Olmsted plan, actual construction did not start until 1912. In 1918 nearly half of the park was given to the state for the military academy The Citadel.

The period from 1925 until 1955 was the park's Golden Age. Azaleas, dogwoods, camellias, crape myrtles, roses, and wisterias enticed residents to stroll and picnic in the park. But by the 1960s operating funds were strained and Hampton Park fell into disrepair. Interest in revitalizing Hampton Park began to grow in the 1980s, and a new master plan was developed that incorporated many of the original Olmsted ideas. The Gazebo Bandstand, the only remaining structure from the 1901 Exposition, was moved across the park to a more appropriate setting, and roses, bulbs, and annuals were planted around its foundation. A 15-bed rose walk was built around the Lagoon and planted mostly with Hybrid Teas and Floribundas.

From the beginning, Hampton Park was planted with roses—some of the earliest photos showed huge rose arbors. When I arrived in 1985, nearly two thousand Hybrid Teas filled the rose walk surrounding the Lagoon. They required spraying, deadheading, and pruning weekly to keep them healthy and blooming, and after four or five years the grafted roses would just give out and need to be replaced.

Previous page: A mixed border with Noisettes at Hampton Park (photo by Les Schwartz)
Left: Vintage postcards showing scenes from old Hampton Park

I began learning about old garden roses and trying to identify roses in a Noisette garden in another park in the downtown area. After talking with countless people, I learned that most of the roses were not Noisettes and that a lady who was an authority on Noisette roses lived in South Carolina. One day I got a call from Frances Parker, my mentor from Beaufort, South Carolina. "I'm coming over and I'm bringing someone to meet you," she said. "I think you two will be great friends." That's how I met Ruth Knopf.

Thanks to Hurricane Hugo most of the roses in that Noisette garden were washed away, so we were able to replace the Teas and Chinas with Noisettes, all of which did beautifully without the extra care that we were giving the Hybrid Teas in Hampton Park. Having learned about the old Teas and Chinas in that Noisette garden, I began to lobby my director to replace all of the roses in the Hampton Park Rose Walk with old Teas, Chinas, Polyanthas, Noisettes, and shrub roses, and got the okay about the same time that we began to plan the Noisette Rose Study.

The Noisette Rose Study

As planning for the 9th International Heritage Rose conference took off, Ruth proposed that we make this conference not only memorable but educational. The planners decided to introduce conference attendees to the Noisette roses, the first class of rose hybridized in America, right here in Charleston. Lively discussions followed. Was there anything new to be learned about these roses? Besides Ruth, who were the Noisette experts? Where were the roses to be found so that we could visit and compare them? These and many other questions cropped up. In the end an educational goal emerged: to collect the Noisettes in one spot, and to observe and compare them.

We needed to find a space that was large enough to plant all the roses we collected, and that had average-to-rich soil and easy access to water for irrigation. To educate not only conference attendees but locals, the space would also need to offer unlimited public access. When plans for locating the Noisette Study on private land fell through, my director gave permission to use Hampton Park, which met all the space, soil, water, and public access requirements. And especially satisfying to me was the fact that Philippe Noisette's Rose Nursery had been located about four blocks north of the park.

The next task—collecting roses for the study—was daunting. Ruth and several knowledgeable rose people put together a list of Noisettes and sent out requests for Noisette donations to nurseries and individuals with rare Noisettes. As the roses arrived, they were planted in groups of three in the Hampton Park Rose Walk beds. Each hole was prepared with our special rose planting recipe. As the date of the con-

Hampton Park (photo by Les Schwartz)

ference approached, I worried about the empty look of the beds with their young roses, so annuals and perennials were added.

Several roses were destroyed by Formosan termites, which eat live wood. Hampton Park is full of them, and rose wood seems to be tasty. The rose

shipment from overseas was held in customs too long and the roses were black when we picked them up. Only one rose survived and it turned out not to be a Noisette!

Then Gregg Lowery arrived and our real work began. We counted petals, stamens, and buds, and then described to the letter how each flower looked, smelled, and felt. It was a treat to have an expert explain all aspects of the rose you held in your hand.

It never occurred to me that we would do more than press specimens, but then came Dr. Malcolm Manners and the DNA comparisons.

The conference and its focus on the Noisettes shed new light on this class of roses and stimulated interest in them. Since our Noisette Study Garden began, several other public places have collected and planted these lovely, hardy old roses. ✑

Hampton Park's Volunteer Program

n the spring of 2001, we finished planting the collection of Noisettes for the Noisette Study only to find that while the roses flourished, they needed to be underplanted with annuals and perennials to set off their beauty and fill in our beds. We also added Teas, Chinas, and Polyanthas to complement the Noisettes. I have always agreed with Mike Shoup's philosophy that you should have roses in your garden, not just a garden of roses. Knowing that the roses would require constant care, we figured that removing all of the flowers would give us great new blooms in six weeks—a bloom cycle that we could count on. The annual and perennial bloom cycles varied, so they required more attention to keep them looking their best.

With the increased workload leading up to the 9th International Heritage Rose Conference, the Horticulture Division was stretched thin until Valerie Perry, Associate Director of Museums with the Historic Charleston Foundation, took a lunch tour of Hampton Park with her employees. A resident of one of the neighborhoods near Hampton Park, Valerie has a vested interest in what goes on here. When she learned how understaffed we were, Valerie offered to pull together a volunteer group to help on Saturday mornings to prepare the park for the conference.

For the three months before the conference, Valerie and another neighborhood leader, Les Schwartz, recruited enough volunteers to keep the beds weeded, watered, pruned, and deadheaded. The success of this effort inspired me to create the Volunteer Program, which is now thriving with over sixty volunteers. Also thriving is the bed adoption program, which gives citizens and local businesses an opportunity to design, plant and maintain a piece of this historic park and to contribute to its rich history. Without the volunteers and all the community support, Hampton Park would not be the civic and horticultural treasure that it is today.

'Mme Alfred Carrière' (photo by Étienne Bouret)

ant Noisettes, 'Mme Alfred' has a quiet, classy disposition, being soft blush pink to white. She also has a perfume which befits such a delightful lady. When you add to this her continuity of flower from June to November and her lush clothing of greyish-green foliage, she deserves to be in every garden.

As well as all the aforementioned attributes, as though they are not enough, she is also very undemanding in cultivation terms. Like all roses she will benefit from an annual feeding in the spring and is better left unsprayed by chemicals. Just the occasional splash of mildly soapy water will keep the aphids at bay.

It is widely known that the beautiful group of roses called the Noisettes prefer the warmer parts of the world, but there is one which has proved itself extremely hardy here in my native county of Norfolk in the UK. It is the lovely 'Mme Alfred Carrière'. Not only is this old climbing rose one of the hardiest of the Noisettes, but it is also one of the most versatile for use anywhere in the garden. Although, of course, there are more flamboy-

If 'Mme Alfred Carrière' has enough space to romp away, she could easily cover a sizeable wall, but if her exuberance has to be tamed she will not object to being contained within a smaller space or on obelisks or arches. She will also tolerate considerable shade.

—Peter Beales

CHAPTER NINE

Charleston's Heritage Rose Trail

Ruth Knopf

I N THE HISTORIC CITY of Charleston, South Carolina, a new walk of old roses winds around the whole peninsula of residential and commercial streets. Through churchyards and cemeteries, municipal gardens and historic house gardens, beside grand public buildings and across schoolyards, down alleys and along hidden pedestrian passageways that are as old as Charleston itself, this pathway of roses celebrates the old roses that thrive in the Lowcountry.

The idea for this rose walk began germinating several years before the 9th International Heritage Rose Conference of 2001. In the 1980s, local citizens started rediscovering the old roses of their city. A few brave souls who loved the Tea, China, and Noisette roses that were so enduring in Carolina gar-

*Previous page: Unitarian Church with 'Maréchal Niel'
cascading along the fence (photo by Ruth Knopf)*
Above: 'Maréchal Niel' (photo by Malcolm Manners)
Right: Cathedral of St. John the Baptist (photo by Ruth Knopf)

tarian Church and elsewhere throughout the city. Also, plantings at some of Charleston's finest historic homes, like the Nathaniel Russell House, were revised to reflect what might have been grown in the eighteenth and nineteenth centuries.

The idea soon arose of adorning Charleston with the Noisette roses that had played such a part in the city's history and of establishing a "Noisette Trail" that would showcase the rose that had become so well known and loved around the world. A group of gardeners who were engaged in the planning of the 9th International Heritage Rose Conference of 2001 became determined to link together these good beginnings with an ambitious wander through the roses of the city. They raised money to purchase many hundreds of rose plants and grew cuttings from existing old roses in Charleston and from rose foundlings gathered by collectors like myself from all over the Carolinas. These historic roses came from all over the country, and many were donated by nurseries and other old rose collectors.

Now nearly every neighborhood of the city includes a section of the Heritage Rose Trail, from the College of Charleston to the Battery and back up to Anson Street. The rose trail stretches far afield from the old city to include the repository of Noisette roses at Hampton Park and the gardens of Boone Hall Plantation where I had planted one of the first extensive collections of old Southern roses in the area.

dens knew these roses belonged back in Charleston. Some had survived in old cemeteries and in the gardens that had not been remade in the 1930s. The first humble Noisettes, 'Champneys' Pink Cluster' and 'Blush Noisette', have a simple eighteenth-century charm that seemed appropriate to the elegance of this historic American city. With thoughtful planning, old climbing Noisettes began to embellish the old iron palings in historic churchyards at the Uni-

Where not long ago old roses clung to life in just a few stray corners, Charleston is now awash in them and their legacy is preserved. Roses like the beautiful creamy yellow "Tradd Street Climber" are no longer sole survivors but rather multiply their fragrant garlands down many lanes and alleyways. Throughout the city's historic sites, the Heritage Rose Trail map greets visitors and leads them to the roses.

Left: St. Philip's Episcopal Church
Above: 'Blush Noisette'
Right: Joseph Manigault House (photos by Ruth Knopf)

'Crépuscule' in a private garden in South West Australia (photo by Odile Masquelier)

I must choose 'Crépuscule' (French for *twilight*) as my favorite Noisette. In our hot dry climate, with a 10-inch rainfall supplemented by irrigation, 'Crépuscule' is quite evergreen. Its foliage is mid to dark green and ample, and the bushes will build up to 9 to 12 feet in time. Flowers have only about 15 to 25 petals, but the buds, which open to show golden stamens, are apricot-gold and shapely. I have never seen any disease whatsoever on any bush of 'Crépuscule'.

'Crépuscule' is excellent for arches and hedges or in a bower, and also as a background for a garden seat because it has very few thorns. Easily the best of all roses as a weeper on a tall standard, it may take several years to reach the ground. Spectacular in the spring flush, it then repeats through summer and autumn and into winter. Pruning is minimal. The flowers fade in the summer heat but then regain their rich color during autumn.

A free-standing hedge of fifty bushes lining a road leading to a sheep stud in New South Wales on the Murrumbidgee River is a glorious sight in spring. A garden here in our town of Renmark has a weeping specimen at either side of the front door, and bushes are only cut back enough for people to go into the house! As I write this in the beginning of August, there are still clusters of flowers. What more could you ask for in a rose?

—**David Ruston, South Australia**

Selected Bibliography

CHAPTER ONE: *Charleston in the Age of John Champneys*

Cothran, James R. *Gardens of Historic Charleston.* Columbia: University of South Carolina Press, 1995.

Linder, Suzanne Cameron. *Historical Atlas of the Rice Plantations of the Ace River Basin—1860.* Columbia: South Carolina Department of Archives and History, 1995.

Rogers, George C., Jr. *Charleston in the Age of the Pinckneys.* Columbia: University of South Carolina Press, 1969/1980.

Rosen, Robert. *A Short History of Charleston.* San Francisco: Lexikos Press, 1982.

CHAPTER FIVE: *Catalogue of the Old Noisettes*

Lowery, Gregg, and Phillip Robinson. *Vintage Gardens Book of Roses.* Sebastopol: Vintage Gardens, 2005.

Proceedings of the 9th International Heritage Rose Conference. Dallas: The Heritage Rose Foundation, 2001. To order, go to www.heritagerosefoundation.org.

CHAPTER SIX: *The Hampton Park Noisette Study*

Frederick, C., A. Wagner, and N. Morvillo. 2002. "Randomly Amplified Polymorphic DNA (RAPD) Analysis of the Musk Roses (*Rosa moschata*)." *Proceedings of the Florida State Horticultural Society* 115:117–119

Lewis, A., M. Caroniti, and N. Morvillo. 2004. "Investigating the Identity of Rose Varieties Utilizing Randomly Amplified Polymorphic DNA (RAPD) Analysis." *Proceedings of the Florida State Horticultural Society* 117:312–316.

Manners, Malcolm M., N. Morvillo, C. Frederick, and A. Wagner. 2004. "RAPD-PCR Answers Some Long-standing Questions about Rose Identification." *Acta Horticulturae* 634:85–89.

Manners, Malcolm M. 2001. "A Brief Explanation of DNA Analysis, and Specifically, RAPD Analysis, as Used in the Florida Southern College Rose Studies." *Proceedings of the 9th International Heritage Rose Conference,* 35–39.

———. "DNA Studies on the Musk Rose at Florida Southern College, Lakeland, FL." *Proceedings of the 9th International Heritage Rose Conference,* 40–41.

———. 2001. "Research on the Early Noisettes: DNA Analysis at Florida Southern College of Roses at the Hampton Park Study Garden." *Proceedings of the 9th International Heritage Rose Conference,* 46–48.

Wagner, A., C. Frederick, and N. Morvillo. 2002. "Investigation of the Origin of 'Champney's Pink Cluster', 'Blush Noisette', and 'Napoleon' Roses Using Randomly Amplified Polymorphic DNA (RAPD) Analysis." *Proceedings of the Florida State Horticultural Society* 115:120–122.

CHAPTER SEVEN: *France and the Tea-Noisettes*

Amat, Charles, ed. *Les plus belles roses au début du 20ème siècle.* Paris: Société Nationale d'Horticulture de France, 1912.

Boitard, Camozet, Cels, Doverges, Jacques, Jacquin, Lemon, E. Martin, Neumann, Louis Noisette and Pepin. *Journal et flore des jardins.* Paris: Rousselon Libraire-Editeur, 1832.

Catalogue descriptif des espèces variétés et sous variétés du genre rosier cultivées chez Prévost Fils. Rouen: Nicétas Periaux Le Jeune, 1829.

Curtis, Henry. *Beauties of the Rose.* Bristol: John Lavars, 1850–1853.

Dickerson, Brent C. *Roll Call: The Old Rose Breeder.* iUniverse, 2000.

Jamain, H., and E. Forney. *Les roses.* Paris: Rothschild, 1873.

Loiseleur Deslongchamps, J. L. A. *La rose: Son histoire, sa culture, sa poesie.* Paris: Audot, 1844.

Paquet, Martin Victor. *Choix des plus belles roses.* Paris: Chez Dusacq, 1854.

Parsons, S. B. *The Rose: Its History, Poetry, Culture and Classification.* New York: Wiley & Putnam, 1847.

Paul, William. *The Rose Garden.* London: Kent and Co., 1878 and 1903.

Redouté, P. J., C. A. Thory, Gisèle de La Roche, and Gordon D. Rowley. *Les roses.* Antwerp: De Schutter, 1974–1978.

Contributors

Peter Beales, managing director of Peter Beales Roses Limited in the UK, is the author of numerous classics of rose literature, including *Roses, Visions of Roses, Twentieth-Century Roses,* and *Classic Roses.*

JoAnn Breland, Superintendent of Horticulture for the City of Charleston, South Carolina, has supervised plant production, installation, and maintenance in public areas throughout the city for 22 years. One of the original eight founding members of the Charleston Horticultural Society, she also founded and leads the City of Charleston Garden Club.

Mimi Cathcart was the chairman of the 9th International Heritage Rose Conference, which was held in Charleston, South Carolina in 2001.

Liesbeth Cooper, a former president of The Bermuda Rose Society, received the 2006 World Rose Award from the World Federation of Rose Societies for her work in preserving old Bermuda roses and tracing their heritage.

Gwen Fagan, author of *Roses at the Cape of Good Hope,* was awarded a gold medal in 1992 from the Simon van der Stel Foundation for her contribution to the conservation of South Africa's historic gardens and architecture.

C. Patton Hash was born in Hattiesburg, Mississippi, on May 24, 1965, and raised in Birmingham, Alabama. After serving in the U.S. Navy, he moved to Charleston and worked as a tour guide for Old South Carriage and in various capacities at the South Carolina Historical Society. He later lived in Washington, D.C. before returning to Birmingham, where he died in 2005 at the age of 39.

Virginia Kean is a freelance writer, editor, and producer based in the San Francisco Bay Area. In 2005 she cofounded *Rosa Mundi,* the journal of the Heritage Rose Foundation, and is its editor in chief.

Ruth Knopf is South Carolina's greatest promoter of growing old roses, especially Teas and Noisettes. After ten years as head gardener at Boone Hall Plantation, she is now a consulting garden designer for them and other private and public gardens. In 2005, she was the first recipient of the Charleston Horticultural Society's prestigious 1830 Award for her contributions to Charleston's horticultural heritage.

Gregg Lowery, vice president of publications for the Heritage Rose Foundation, owns Vintage Gardens, a California-based mail-order rose nursery whose collection of over 3,500 varieties from every rose class is the largest offered by any nursery in the world. He is the coauthor of *Vintage Gardens Book of Roses.*

Malcolm M. Manners is professor of citrus and environmental horticulture at Florida Southern College, where he directs the college's rose mosaic virus heat therapy program and manages a collection of more than three hundred rose varieties. A past chairman of the American Rose Society's committees on rose registration and classification, he is a trustee of the Heritage Rose Foundation.

Odile Masquelier of Lyon, France, founded the first French old rose society, Roses Anciennes en France. Her garden, La Bonne Maison, attracts visitors from around the world and is featured in Mirabel Osler's *Secret Gardens of France* and in Peter Beales' *Vision of Roses.* Her book, *La Bonne Maison, Un Jardin de Roses Anciennes,* was published in French by Flammarion in 2001.

John Meffert, former director of the Preservation Society of Charleston, is a lecturer and study leader for the National Trust for Historic Preservation, the Smithsonian Institution, and Colonial Williamsburg. He is the author of two books on the history of Charleston: *An Album from the Charleston Museum Collection* and *Photographs from the Avery Research Center.*

Roger Phillips is a renowned author, pioneering color photographer of plants, and broadcaster based in the UK. His more than 20 books include *Roses* and *The Quest for the Rose,* both coauthored with botanist Martyn Rix. His website is www.rogersrose.com.

David Ruston, a former president of the World Federation of Rose Societies, is the founder of Ruston's Roses in Renmark, South Australia. His many awards include the Order of Australia Medal for services to horticulture (1982) and the Dean Hole Medal of the Royal National Rose Society (1994).

William (Bill) C. Welch is a professor of horticulture at Texas A&M University in College Station, Texas. His books include *Antique Roses for the South* and *The Southern Heirloom Garden.*

Barbara Worl, owner of Sweetbrier Press, is the publisher of a facsimile edition of *Beauties of the Rose* by Henry Curtis. Her garden in Menlo Park, California was featured in *Visions of Roses* by Peter Beales.

Index

In this index, the common names of the roses are in Roman type; scientific names are in italics. Bold page numbers indicate photos or illustrations.